Thailand
1997
December

They say the best way to a man's heart is through his stomach.

We say the best way to enjoy a country is through her culture.

Sawasdee Ralph (and) Charlotte —

The "manners and customs" of Thailand may raise eyebrows, but will give you a few laughs, too.

Merry Christmas Love!

BB
Publication

DOs &
DON'Ts
IN THAILAND

W9-CHF-285

DOs & DON'Ts IN THAILAND
2nd Revised Edition 1995

Publisher
Pranom Supavimolpum

Text by
Kenny Yee
Catherine Gordon

Cover & Illustrations by
Han Tun
Minual
San Win

Printed in Thailand by
Amarin Printing and Publishing Public Company Limited.

Copyright© 1995 Book Promotion & Service Ltd.
ISBN: 974-89009-8-3

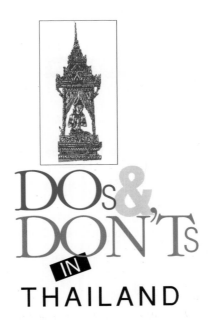

DOs & DON'Ts IN THAILAND

Contents

PART 2 : AROUND AND ABOUT

INTRODUCTION

This second edition has been expanded to a greater depth on those topics that are of wider interest to the general reader, especially to new-comers.

It has also been extended to include changes arising from the rapid economic and hence, social, progress of Bangkok; though not of Thailand, per se.

DO...READ THIS BOOK with a very open mind. It states what should be done in a given situation and recommends some alternatives.

DON'T...FEEL OFFENDED with our suggestions. They are meant to help the reader better understand Thai society as a whole and not to belittle anyone or any social norm of any culture.

This book highlights those most likely aspects of Thai culture and general situations that one is likely to encounter. It should prove useful for those who are not quite as yet conversant with the plurality of Thai society. It is not an academic exercise to embody everything.

This is, hopefully, a handy 'mini-manual' for a quick search to pertinent areas of Thai customs on what should be done, or not to be done, when in the company of Thai people to ensure a congenial and therefore happy relationship. This is the main aim of the book.

Those suggestions on what ought *not* to be done could prove to be eye-opening. If remembered and followed, a non-Thai would not offend his local host. The foreigner would be elated to know that even if an action is not done properly, or a word spoken awkwardly, it will always be pleasing to the typical Thai.

Obviously, the foreigner needs to adjust to a situation at perhaps some inconvenience to him or her. It will be found also that many locals will try very hard to accommodate and even tolerate some 'strange' foreign mannerisms, speech and outlook. For everyone to be happy, the traffic should be two-way. The Thais know this; it's up to the foreigner. Note that it can be exasperating in the beginning!

THE TWIN PILLARS OF THAI SOCIETY

Thais are not difficult to please. They are an easy-going people, usually minding their own business and going about their daily chores without fuss or complaint. This makes them warm and friendly.

However, arising out of this apparent semi-complacency, two currently outstanding aspects are noticeable: '*mai pen rai*' and '*chai yen yen.*'

'MAI PEN RAI'

This is a howler to the Westerner! The English equivalent is "never mind," "it's o.k.," "not at all," or "no problem." Anyone who has moved around a bit here would have heard this phrase at least once if not several times over.

In an awkward or urgent situation, it can be irritating by western concept, but one has to understand the Thai way of looking at things, which can appear to be more practical in many instances. Let's suppose there's a man brooding by a river bank; a Thai man walks up and upon finding out that the man has just lost his fiance, the local would probably say 'never mind' instead of 'I know how you must feel; take it easy.'

This phrase is, if you like, equivalent to it's no use crying over spilt milk. It has a very calming effect, not to be confused with giving up.

'CHAI YEN YEN'

The figurative meaning would be "take it easy," "calm down," or "control yourself" when one's blood pressure has risen and is about to be translated into a verbal outburst or tantrum. It is normally used when one is emotionally upset and anxious.

The origins could have stemmed from the fact that Thailand had been and, still is, mainly an agricultural country. Today, the majority are still attached to tilling the earth and they have to accept what nature provides or removes; so, what is the use of getting upset, fighting and swearing on the elements? If it takes twenty minutes to change a flat tyre, it takes twenty minutes to change a flat tyre. Getting hot headed, cursing the pebble, or kicking the car would not make any difference to the mechanics of replacement. On the contrary, the hot headed person loses out to himself.

The ability to maintain calmness and the willingness to understand another's difficulty and thereby easing him of his guilt or embarrassment is a classic social etiquette in the Kingdom. Here's a simple example:

You and your friend are hopelessly stuck in a traffic jam, causing you to be definitely late for an appointment. You fume like a chimney and look like the bull about to charge the matador. You give a sideway glance to your friend. He smiles (!) and coos 'mai pen rai' (!!). Finally, you made it for the appointment, some two,- three hours late. You, the typical *farang,* apologised profusely, blaming everything and everyone, including yourself. Finally, when your one-man vaudeville is over, your Thai friend simply smiles and says: *mai pen rai.*

You might be surprised and you might ask, "You mean you are not *angry?*" (You can almost see his answer in the air).

Do try to remember that nearly all Thais are genuinely happy to befriend and help visitors, which cannot be said for many other countries. Thailand **is** unique in hospitality terms; one has to experience to understand. But at the same time no one would like to be offended, especially relating to revered customs and habits. This is important to bear in mind from the very beginning. With exceptions, Thais can be deadly if seriously offended and/or pushed to a corner. Who would not? The point to keep in mind is not to exert superiority because the visitor happens to be richer, more 'educated' or bigger physically. For instance, one does not shout at a janitor or labourer even if no one is within ear-shot. It is simply not done in this country.

Respect begets respect. The overall aim of this book is to ensure that the *foreign reader will maintain his dignity in the eyes of the ordinary Thai.* This point is essential for a happy and fruitful stay.

The final aim of **Do's & Dont's** is that if one has an idea or two or some background information on how to avoid possible unpleasantness, one could perhaps save one's self from probable discomfort and embarrassment; maybe even from bodily harm.

Towards this end, some areas that are not specifically habits of culture have been included. These are idiosyncrasies arising out of a fast developing country that sadly destroy some truly admirable aspects of tradition. In any country, when rural folks move to big cities and pick up city habits, the very same folks may surprise even their own parents later.

And Bangkok is a city of many ex-rural folks.

This book then hopes to bridge the gap of lack of understanding of the local by the foreigner.

PART 1

IMPORTANT BACKGROUND

This part contains the main cultural aspects of Thai society.

THE THAI PERSON
THE RELIGION
THE MONARCHY

The more prominent.......

CHARACTER TRAITS

The Thais as a group display certain behavioral traits that are more pronounced than many other societies as a population. Even among Southeast Asians, they stand out differently in mentality and body language.

This is due in part to the recognition of all local residents as THAIS regardless of race or origin. Many residents who became permanent citizens find that assimilation into Thai ways is smooth and hardly noticeable, particularly if one is espoused to a local: one sort of become 'Thai' and ending up often speaking pidgin English even when in non-Thai company. Such is the impact of 'Thaism.' Other factors also influence the population to fuse so many groups into one harmoniously.

One of these is religion, more specifically, Buddhism. Most ethnic locals are Buddhist. The multiplicity of temples, the ever presence of monks, the fact that a monk will almost always give an audience to any follower almost anytime of his free hours helps to bind the unseen cord of togetherness.

Another is early school day activities in the poor provinces. The "activities" typically consist of making repairs to buildings, weeding plots of flower beds, toilet cleaning, compound maintenance, even paving potholes where needed. Such co-operative discipline cultivates closeness and indirectly, preservation of learned values. Born into initial suffering, a young Thai grows up to appreciate ethics: respect, gentleness, caring and a host of other human home values.

Unfortunately, with industrial advancement and spiralling cities, and 'bad western influence' via the media, exceptions will have to be made for any statement today.

THE PLUS SIDE

PATIENCE

I t is an exception to come across a Thai without patience. Thais display a commendable amount of this quality. It is not surprising that psychologists and psychiatrists are not rich here.

While many an outsider would be fuming (and probably swearing away privately) a local will simply smile and continue to wait for something to materialise, however long it takes. Failing materialisation, he/she will usually call it off without complaining. We won't see Thais putting on disgusting looks at a long check-out counter or while waiting for a take home order to be ready. Certainly, whatever his upbringing, he will never take it out on the cashier with, "Why did it take so long?" or similar interjections so common elsewhere.

It is obvious there are demerits to excessive patience but we are not talking about pros and cons of any element in this book. We are trying to emphasise outstanding aspects of local life for anyone new to blend in or not to get headlong into.

TOLERANCE

Thais have the beautiful capacity of tolerating inconveniences for long periods and at great suffering sometimes, such as standing all the way on a long distance overnight bus trip. They do not complain about too much work or not enough time. A Thai man will not demand to be explained why a project takes so long. For instance, electricity breaks down, he phones for reinstallation, the department sends a team that takes two or even three days to reset the job. Well, the Thai would bear with it. He might even defend the time lag with: "it's a dangerous job, "the workers know best." In no way will he utter, "look at those loafers."

Meantime? He might resort to candles, lamps, whatever. He might even joke that the traffic congestion makes it troublesome for them to work, to run up and down getting spares.

There will be that fellow who is a company's executive living in some high-rise expensive condo who has brought back some tenets of impatience from his overseas university life. Here we are not talking of people in this category, who do not represent the majority. But even then, he will revert subconsciously to his good true self should he go upcountry for vacation.

The typical working modern Thai has a split personality in Bangkok and in other tourist towns where he is more conscious of money, greed, status and selfishness.

DO EXERCISE TOLERANCE when going about the country, particularly when it comes to ordering food, waiting for change, expecting an errand to be done or even when trying to pay a bill.

DO NOT RUSH a worker or complain to his superior behind his back. That will be unwise. It is better to explain clearly, repeat the instruction and maybe say it for a third time if it is complicated and then stand back and wait... (and hope!).

DO NOT BE UPSET...Expect it (whatever *it* is) to be done in a longer time than where you come from. Do give plenty of allowance so that if it should be done inside your set time period, and there are surprises, you will save a few more hairs from dropping. (If you happen to have no hair, well...from getting a few extra facial wrinkles?).

TEMPER

With patience and tolerance forming two 'props' it is no wonder to find that Thais do not easily lose their heads at anything or everything that many outsiders may find irritating or frustrating.

This has elevated to the degree that to lose one's temper amounts to being unbecoming of the person, namely, a person of 'low' character or poor upbringing. This permeates in privacy as well as in public.

DO NOT (no, **TRY** not to) LOSE your temper at all. Ha! Easier said than done. Controlling temper is like giving up cigarettes. It's either done, for good, or not at all. Many Thais have not so much as raise their voice when angry, let alone bellow out their temper. This is very pronounced in the countryside. In fact, they often speak so softly, amounting to a whisper that one wonders if anything is wrong with their throats.

CALMNESS

There is no secret, it would seem. It's simply an extension of all the above ingredients combined. What the Thais have is the ability to preserve and utilise these good social customs without being artificial about it. The western man may be a saint while he is out dining and socialising among the elite but when he gets home, he becomes the opposite to his own family, even before he has fully undressed. The Thai, while not appearing to be so loving and caring (exhibited by hand-or and waste holding, an arm over the shoulder, etc) maintains a steady level of comfortable compromise to his friends and to himself. Put another way, the western behaviour can be sweet but deceptive while that of the Thai is crude but straightforward. There is no hard feeling if he forgets to kiss his wife before he goes to work. He does not do this anyway, so both are comfortable.

In a car accident or a natural catastrophe, you will not find those affected running about like lunatics and yelling their heads off with wild gestures. Thais do not create a scene out of a mishap, regardless of whose fault. They have been brought up to keep their cool, to keep their heads in place under distress.

This has the negative spin off in greeting when it comes to seeing a long lost friend. It becomes a matter-of-fact meeting, at most a big smile and a battery of questions, no hugs, no kisses, no back slapping. It can make you wonder whether he is really glad to see you like he says. So then, do not be disappointed.

DO NOT FEEL let down if you have done a favour for a Thai and he does not seem to bodily express his thanks.

DO NOT HUG a Thai if the position is the other way round and you want to boisterously show him your appreciation. In Thailand, a firm "Thank you very much" is the norm. Even if your intentions are good and clean, he will not like it. The good thing about this custom is that nobody can hug your wife for whatever reason!

It follows that it is almost next to impossible to be engaged in a violent argument with a local: he will just smile or back away. Though some can be treacherous or dangerous like all human beings, Thais are nearly all the time, calm, gentle and polite.

We discount here the occasional bar brawl a foreigner might get into with a local.

THE MINUS SIDE

SENSITIVITY

For some unexplained reason, Thais are ultra sensitive by outside standard, so that even jokes could cause some embarrassment or displeasure to them. It is thus difficult for a western extrovert to joke with his local counterpart even though both may be long-time acquaintances. The Thai simply cannot take it.

One cannot say to a Thai for instance, "You can never make it to the top if you work like this. Why don't you find something more suitable, eh?" Such a remark is an insult and amounts to belittling him, not a joke or a challenge for him to prove otherwise. Should there be others about, you would have just made him 'lose face.'

This makes it touchy to be candid and encourages one to speak only that which should be spoken. It makes the atmosphere very uneasy and unrelaxing, tense sometimes. A Thai will have no second thought in dropping a friendship over a misunderstanding.

This aspect robs off the fun at a picnic and blots out the glow at a beach party, but that's it.

It goes to mean also that if a male Caucasian carelessly say 'I like you very much' to a Thai lady, she can misconstrue this to mean he loves her and before very long, it could be parents visiting time! This could be the second step to staging a stag party if he is not careful. Before long, he condemns himself to giving up his singularity, all because of one not understanding the other and the other so sensitive as to misread an expression.

DO ADAPT TO the Thai way of speech and mannerism as far as possible. To get things across, one has to remodel the line of thinking and importantly, anticipate the effect one's action will have on the local receiving party.

FORGETFULNESS

This is logically related to the Thai's characteristics of patience, tolerance, calmness and general passivity. Semi-complacent, taking it easy and 'why worry about tomorrow' attitude has contributed to certain defects.

Many locals in the catering line seem to have a very shallow retentive memory. Very simple instructions can be forgotten in minutes. Order coffee and two minutes later, the same waiter will return, smile and ask, "Did you say you wanted tea?"

Get the servant to do marketing, the office boy to run an errand or a colleague to buy something along the way and, as sure as the sun will rise, something will go amiss, if not this time, quite surely the next. The most irritating sphere is at restaurants. Urgency, accuracy, quality and responsibility does not exist at a level comparable to the west.

Case in point: Say an importer specifically states in written instructions that all units of an item must carry the stamp of country of origin. The importer from his home country reminds the manufacturer. An acknowledgement is faxed to the worried importer. He now feels relaxed. Good. When the goods finally arrived, guess what happened?

DO NOT EXPECT your verbal instructions to be remembered even if it was written down. This, in Thailand, would be very naive.

DO BE PREPARED to be asked again, however silly you may think.

DO REMEMBER IT is a way of life here. What, forgetfulness? Yes, forgetfulness and also very important, in fact most important of all, is..., is.... (heck, now, I've forgotten what I want to write next! *Mai pen rai;* on to the next point).

UNPUNCTUALITY

Even when there is money to be made, Thais, many times over, simply cannot keep to time. This again is an off-shoot of the plus points. Look at it this way: In the province, time, in terms of hours and minutes, has no relative connotation to a piece of work. "Oh, it will be done in a couple of weeks," or "when the rainy season is over." In Bangkok, with the traffic congestion, it is just next to impossible at most times to keep to a fixed time, in getting to an appointment or movie or restaurant or to go home in the greatest of hurry.

This does not mean Thais will procrastinate automatically. On the other hand, they can be very fast opportunists. They do know how to make hay while the sun shines. Do not underestimate the Thais' brain power!

However, a Thai will simply not uphold an agreement if he does not feel like it. For example, you have a dinner appointment. You are now waiting -and waiting and you have been waiting since waiting time- for him to show up. Finally, he does *not* show up.

Next day, he might offer no apology or felt he had stood you up.

Pressed for an explanation, he said he was in front of his TV and, if he was honest, he did not feel like coming. Why all the fuss? In the other shoe, he will not ask *you* why you failed to turn up. To him, it's over, finished, period. He will accept the let down gracefully. If you try to offer an excuse, his answer will most likely be *"mai pen rai."* (Remember this?)

DO NOT MISTAKEN unpunctuality or slowness of movement to be laziness. They just want to do things in an easy way, which is not the same as

finding an easier way out at the expense of quality. (Have you ever seen a Thai rush-walk the way it is done when after-office workers head toward an underground train station in London or New York?).

THE OTHER SIDE

BANGKOK METROPOLITAN

S ome eight million live, dwell, squat or go unsheltered in a colorful array of accommo dation: high-rise mansions, middle-class con- dos, lower-class apartments, even lower-class thatched huts, no class plank houses and classless makeshifts under hyper highways and anywhere else to avoid the midnight dew.

This lot of people can be divided into three categories for this chapter: original Bangkokians (born, bred and slogging it out in Bangkok); semi-Bangkok residents (permanent opportunists from inside and outside Thailand) and non-Bangkokians (poor country folks from faraway provinces who came voluntarily or otherwise for all kinds of reasons).

With such a diverse human conglomeration one can expect all sorts of radiating behaviour from a common habit. So, what to do and what not to do in Bangkok?

Happily and strangely, it is quite easy to get by if a few salient features of the capital are known, but first, a few examples:

A smart-looking lad at a five-star hotel front door greeting you may be living in a slum area. (He would generally be from up-country, as few Bangkok-born lads would opt for such a low paid and low status job). He considers himself lucky, having had a job.

Therefore, he greets you warmly. He is humble, having gone to school for maybe only four years as his parents are too poor to let him continue.

He might have to send whatever is left of his little pay to his mum and dad. His disposition molds his character. You feel good and proclaim Bangkok is so friendly, even the bell boy...

Next, you embark on a conducted tour in a gleaming air-conditioned coach.

You ask the smartly-dressed stewardess a question. She answers without that warm smile you were told is so predominating in Thailand.

You ask another question. No answer.

Worse, she just glides by. She has other things to do than answering questions, dumb or acceptable.

She is from Bangkok, probably university educated, attended P.R. courses and is efficient in her work. She may come from a well-to-do family.

So, if these examples represent the good and poor side of life in Bangkok, how do we know when is what? We don't. But we can always remember to lend the locals extra elbow room for their lower standard of living, different perception of good manners and more limited exposure to experience and *finesse*.

Many Thais have never been out of the country and have only a shallow grasp of what the world is. Many respect a foreigner who is seen as a more educated and smarter person and so these many are eager to help. This stems from their childhood upbringing when little children must help out at home, around the temple and in the neighbourhood. But largely, this was yesterday.

Today, the same helpful person will still help but for a more different reason: $$$! It follows that there are many Dr Jeckells and Mr Hydes in Bangkok. It would be an occasion rather than a tradition for a good chap to turn into a bad guy to make your experience ugly.

The most important point to remember is to bear no grudge against the silly fellow, however grievous the incident; after all, it could have been due partly to your fault also, whatever you may say. If this is acceptable, then it will be most fruitful to proceed with how what goes on in Bangkok, the City of Angels.

DO NOT EXPECT any sense of urgency or responsibility to be at par with your level. Remember *mai pen rai* and *chai yen yen?* Thais are, by and large, happy-go-lucky and unless something appeals to them very much, that is, it is *sanuk* or pleasant to do, they will take their own time and do it in their own way, even if you should be the boss. (They now have an added reason: traffic. Bangkok's vehicular jams should be in the Guiness Book of Records. A semi-permanent fourth reason: road flooded, during those wet months of the year. These are excuses for arriving late).

DO NOT THINK that an action or thing is wrong because you have never done or seen it, example: the exotic fruit, durian. (What's wrong with it? Smell- what smell? You mean aroma!)

DO NOT EQUATE Bangkok with Thailand. That would be like saying Chicago is the US or Paris is France. Bangkok the city, the people, the environment and even the way of life does not reflect the total and often romantic reality of this country. Bangkok has a character peculiar all to itself.

DO NOT BELIEVE that all smiles in Bangkok are sincere. Some can be deadly, especially if some well-mannered 'gentleman' strikes up a conversation. Ladies should be more alert. Of course such ill-intent instances occur globally but in Thailand, the total stranger will face a unique problem: language barrier in depth; 'yes/no' is not good enough. You say "yes" and the policeman on beat says "no." Now what?

DO NOT PRESUME the pedestrian has the right of way in the Metropolitan. More people had become 'angels' at zebra-crossings than from snake bites. Everyone is perpetually rushing and, in view of the equally perpetual traffic jams, the bull behind the speeding car has no

time to stop for two-legged zebras. (Unnecessary note: how to cross a zebra then? Easy: look left, look right, look everywhere and then take the overhead pedestrian bridge. A long road to safety is better than a short cut to heaven. By the way, at some overpass, look down, but not at the cars zooming below but to make sure you don't stick one foot onto some hazards or knock into some illegal vendors. One road to be specially treated is Wireless Road with its odd traffic lane flow).

PROVINCIAL PROMINENCE

The Northern and Northeastern parts of Thailand are well noted for their own way of life and in many instances, their warm and genuine hospitality, albeit some untoward incidents can and do happen. Hence, there are some do's and don'ts that can be localised for the provinces that we need not worry about in Bangkok. A visitor, even a long-time resident, can find himself experiencing a new form of culture amazement. Many remote villages still cling to their beliefs and customs -and therefore, expectations- despite Bangkok's swift economic and social changes. Here's what we suggest:

DO REMEMBER THAT these country folks mean well when, for instance, they offer a drink from the same drinking vessel that has already gone round the group in front of your very eyes. You either insist you are not thirsty (and disappoint them) or brace yourself and take a sip or gulp the whole lot down, in which case you might well receive an applause from everyone.(You might also culture shock them instead at not leaving some for the next person; if there is nobody else, by your greedy and rude behaviour).

DO UNDERSTAND THAT many utensils, floor mats and practically everything may not be as clean as you would have wished.

DO TRY TO please your hosts and sit on the floor as they do. They will understand that for westerners, it may require quite a contortive effort to tuck both feet onto one side, akin to the Mermaid of Copenhagen. This often ends up with the foreigner offering stiff competition to the Leaning Tower of Pisa. Most times with obese people, it cannot be done, for long anyway. So, how to sit, for God's sake? Well, force a smile and sit cross-legged, like a popular Buddha statue posture. No decent Thai would adopt this position, especially before a monk but, never mind, the Thais know that not all westerners are civilised. (Unnecessary note: we should consider ourselves lucky that we have chairs to sit on. Herein lies the extreme latent pleasure of visiting rural Thailand. Thais, as a custom, do not sit on chairs or use tables. The Thai words for these two funny things come directly from the Chinese Hokkien/Teochew dialects).

DO NOT FORGET that mosquitoes looking and flying like fighter planes *will,* not may, also extend you a warm welcome even during daylight. At twilight, if you stay overnight, they will be joined by more mosquitoes and insects of all descriptions zooming and attacking like B52s. Do bring some necessities along.

DO TRY TO FEEL at ease when you are ogled at. Everybody from six to sixty years old will stare at strangers. It's like the circus has come to town. Little children who might not have been that close to blond hair or six footers will squat on their haunches, giggle and generally whisper among themselves. Do not be offended; they are not 'back biting.' They are merely curious and simply fascinated because not many new things happen in villages that often. (Approach the youngsters and see what happens).

DO NOT BE alarmed if you find pigs trotting by in front of you, or big, monstrous (perhaps to you) lizards wisping out their forked tongues above your head. In the country, nothing of this sort is alarming amongst the villagers. What would be alarming to them is if some relative, new to Bangkok, got rolled over by an eighteen wheeler.

DO REALISE THAT any way-out province is a different world altogether from Bangkok or high tourist places like Koh Samui, Pattaya, Phuket, Chiang Mai, Hat Yai and the outlying islands like Phi Phi Islands to name the most popular of them, by way of information.

DO BRACE YOURSELF for lots of cultural shocks.

Very important points about....

BODY ATTRIBUTES

This section is specially recommended for anyone to get on amicably with a local.

The casual visitor and first-time tourist should know and remember that Thais place special emphasis on three main body parts: the head, the hands and the feet. A fourth area of relevance for the visitor to know is the entire body: you do not touch a Thai anytime anywhere unless you know him well and there is a spontaneous reflexive action like at the end of a jolly amusing joke. But, to touch a woman on a forearm or any other part during a conversation or at the end of that jolly joke is no joke: it is not polite and will not be accepted. Do it often and you end up losing in many areas.

Most Thais dislike being touched. What about two Thai men holding hands while walking? This is a different story altogether and stamps from various beginnings, like long-time childhood buddies; the bond of tight friendship grows with them and the habit of man-holding-hands together follow along. The other reason is the newly emergence of the gay group.

While we may see female-and-female or, sometimes, male-and-male holding hand gesture, we will seldom see the male-and-female version. Correction: we are seeing more and more nowadays, especially in Bangkok streets. It's the influence of western lifestyle on the younger, usually, university set. If an older couple is so seen, you can be sure the two lovers will feel uncomfortable, with the woman trying to shake the man's hands off. In the west of course, if a woman does that to a chap, he has already become her has-been.

THE HEAD

DO NOT TOUCH ANYONE'S HEAD FOR ANY REASON.

The head is the most important part of the entire body. It should never be touched. Even in jest, you should resist the affectionate casual ruffling of a youngster's hair to show compliments, the way it is done outside Thailand. (Etiquette note: that's why a layman will sit so that his head is lower than that of the monk's; and a younger person will do likewise to an elder person or someone of a higher rank, status or position. The lower the head, the greater the amount of respect given. It is like the Japanese way of bowing in meeting friends).

DO ADVISE A person in advance if you want to remove some fallen article on his hair that gets onto your nerve. Either he does it or he will let you do it. That's about the only time you can touch his head, where good manners are concerned in Thailand. Do it unannounced and you could end up in some intensive care unit!

THE HANDS

DO NOT POINT WITH THE FOREFINGER AT ANYONE.

The hand has two categories: the right being more acceptable and polite when giving or receiving things and putting things into the mouth; the left is generally regarded as of 'lower class' because this fellow is used for cleaning downstairs after toilet duty.

You are left-handed? Gosh!

Answer: Try to remember to use the right hand for giving and receiving things.

In good Thai culture, when receiving something especially from an elder, both hands are used. In the trade, when a shopkeeper receives cash or hands over a receipt, he will offer his right hand with the right elbow supported by his left hand, all in one unbroken graceful movement. This represents a gesture of respect, thankfulness and humility, in this order. No Thai will snatch an article away from the giver's hand. This is totally uncouth to him. It is not done.

Either hand should not be used to point at people, especially the forefinger. Even in a heated argument, let's say, this is not done among Thais. The occasional policeman, from too many TV movies, may use his forefinger to indicate a direction to a tourist but to an elder compatriot, he will automatically refrain from pointing. How does he do it then? He could clasp his right palm with the thumb slightly pointing out, like when we hold a stick.

THE FEET

DO KEEP BOTH FEET ON THE GROUND WHEN SITTING.

The feet are the lowest section of the anatomy, the 'dirtiest' protrusions. They are used for walking and never at pointing.

DO NOT PLACE them such that they inadvertently be pointing towards a person, or religious image or a picture of the Royal Family. The ultimate insult would be to point a foot (or shoe) at somebody's head when referring to him, although he could be at the far corner of a room. Ignore this point and you might just graduate from intensive care to the mortuary!

One can imagine the extreme discomfort of a Thai sitting in a chair with someone else's foot (or feet!) on his backrest, as in a train or cinema. Often, a poor *tuk tuk* driver had to grit his teeth in silence when the tip of some not-so-sweet smelling toes are centimeters from his nape.

(Contradictory note: In some parts of Southern Thailand where aborigines, namely the Sakais, live in jungles and forest fringes, the feet are considered by them to be the most important because they are traditionally hunters and gatherers. No feet, no food. But while they privately adhere to their tribal view, they too follow the Thai concept. They are gradually being assimilated as Thais. In sleeping, their feet are always pointed inwards from the doorway so that no wild animals would have free supper. It all boils down to the question of "nothing is right or wrong but thinking makes it so " really).

THE PERSON

DO NOT STEP OVER ANY PART OF ANOTHER PERSON.

You ou should not step over the person's feet if he/she is sitting up or any part of the body if she/he was lying down.

It will be found that even a Thai boy will not walk over his younger brother's extended legs. That much respect the young lad will extend to his younger sibling.

37

Some unintended such crossings and criss-crossings by foreign backpackers occur almost daily in overnight trains in the third class compartments where at times the coach is sardine-packed. A local will either gently tap the sleeping traveller on the knee or, failing to wake him, would push the legs away to make enough space to squeeze by.

Problem: What happens if, in that train, the sleeping beauty *is* a beauty?

Remember, you cannot touch a lady at any time in public. And a beauty at that!

Suggestion: Get someone who is not asleep to help out or wake up the silly fellow who is snoring to assist. Failing this, use your ingenuity and write to us about it. We just run out of ideas for this!! (You can shout and wake everyone up but we do not recommend this approach. Over to you!).

THE FEMALE BODY

As far as the whole female body goes, you need only to remember two salient points:

DO NOT, in fact, NEVER, touch a local female, friend or otherwise, on any part of the body in public, not even her hand. This is gentlemanliness at its best, not only in Thailand, but across Asian countries. It is taboo. While the male ego still prevails over the female in domestic and office situations, the female is respected. Alas, with night life all over the place, this seems contradictory.

DO NOT TOUCH at all, the second point, your maid servant at home. We would like to repeat this point: Never, never touch the maid, because, do this even with the best of intention and you will give her fears and nightmares **for she can never tell when you are going to touch her again.** Against her upbringing and established principles, you will condemn her to living misery for the rest of her time at your household. And probably in her next housemaid job elsewhere too.

Likewise, it is not a good idea to touch a nurse when she has to perform her duty at your bedside. No excuse can be expected to be accepted. One simply has to forget about 'back home' syndromes.

CLEANLINESS AND SMARTNESS

Thais dress decently and in clean clothes even at home. If you appear unkempt, looking like a 'hippy' and worse still, smelly, do not be surprised if a Thai shies away from you or refuse to greet you with that well-known smile.

It is a sad fact that many outsiders who have stayed here long neglect body and dress hygiene. Thais are way less well-off vis-a-vis foreigners working here yet it can be seen they take great pains to be neat. Look at some tuk tuk/bus drivers. This sense of personal pride is extended to the many hours of patient labour when vendors arrange their basketfuls of cakes and fruits at the roadside.

It will speak well for the foreigner if those roughing it out at cheaper tourist guest houses be smarter-looking when strolling about in department stores and elsewhere.

Thailand's warmest greeting gesture.....

THE 'WAI'

This characteristic Thai way of greeting is one of the most, if not the most, beautiful ways of contact ever 'devised' to promote understanding among human beings.

Done well and gracefully, even for the umpteenth time by the same person to another same person, the one being 'waied' to cannot help but feel a certain warmness for the person 'wai-ing.' Anyone who has been 'wai-ed' to must have felt this sentiment. Many will perhaps agree that it beats the western handshake which at times can look rather sinister. (Grab his hand and you grab a karate chop!).

USAGE

The *wai* is used for several reasons, the most popular being to express a hearty 'welcome' or 'hello.' When it is intended as this form of greeting, the greeter almost always smiles and says "sawatdee" while lowering the head slightly or, in the case of females, executing a slight courtesy as well.

It would be most impolite *not* to return a *wai* greeting, akin to rejecting an intended handshake. In fact, rejecting a handshake is not as debase as not acknowledging a wai. A wai is often an outward sign of recognising a standing of higher status to the person being 'wai'ed' to. Not to acknowledge a *wai* is unpardonable and speaks extremely poorly of the person. The exception for the ordinary person concerns Their Majesties and monks who do not *wai* back to anyone by virtue of position and religious stature.

However, it is not compulsory to return a *wai* with a *wai* under various situations but it must still be acknowledged even if one might not feel like it. It's the thing to do, not what one feels one wants to do. It's social etiquette, good manners, respecting the other party, displaying acceptance and everything else all rolled into one. A superior could acceptably return a subordinate's *wai* with a nod, a smile, a lifted finger or just a grunting noise but he must react.

Apart from the sheer sign of greeting, the *wai* is simultaneously a sign of respect for an elder or a person of a higher status regardless of sex. Thus a well brought up child would *wai* his or her parents upon returning from school; an office boy would *wai* his superior immediately upon going into the boss's room. He would not do it daily but he certainly would if the boss has important guests. It's a mark of protocol to show the boy respects his boss; a guest would *wai* his elder host upon entering the house, but a younger host would *wai* a visiting elder first.

WHEN TO WAI

When to *wai* therefore depends on the relationship of the two people. Who should *wai* first depends on the relative social status of the parties. The *wai* carries the inward sign of the person 'wai-ing' that he acknowledges the superiority of the person he is 'wai-ing.' Where two people are of equal status, then common sense dictates that the person who is leaving a party of friends should excuse himself by 'wai-ing' everybody. There is no 'loss of face' in this case but sheer good manners.

A Westerner would go a long way to being respected when he does a *wai* to an elder person or one of higher status. But he should not *wai* one inferior to him occupationally. This would tantamount to misuse. Whereas a Caucasian father would extend his hand to his young child and say "hello there, son," in Thai society, the father never *wai* his children first. He does not even *wai* his wife first. Such is the symbolic strength of status order.

A Westerner should never *wai* first to a waiter, tailor, vendor, domestic help or a taxi driver even if he/she is younger than them all. The fact that the Westerner is paying for service makes him the boss.

ORIGIN?

Merely for reading pleasure it might be amusing
to make a comparison of two neighbouring
countries as this question could be a tough
one to answer. The 'wai' is strikingly similar in gesture
to the Indian *'namase'* greeting when the palms are
clasped in front of the body. Historically, India was
one country that had great influences on Thai customs
and aspects of religion. China was another country
that had exerted its cultural influences on Thailand.
The Chinese way of greeting, *'koh kung'* also involves
joining two hands in front of the body but the Indian
way is closest to the Thai *wai*.

Religiously, one of the many poses of the
Buddha shows him clasping both hands together. A
sign of peace. Could this be the origin of the 'origin'?
What do you think? Perhaps you might know more
certainly than we do.

POSITIONS OF THE *WAI*

The illustrations show the two most common variations of the *wai* greeting. Figure A is the normal *wai*. Figure B is the *wai* to a superior. Note the differences of the positions of the clasped palms and the directions of look. Figure C is the *wai* that one executes to convey the warmest of respect, acknowledgement or thankfulness.

One important point to note is that the courteous way to show respect is to lower the head and body slightly. It can be seen that some Thais lower their bodies so much that they seem to be looking for a fallen coin on the ground.

Figure (A)

Figure (B)

Figure (C)

HERE'S A BRAIN TWISTER TO TEST UNDERSTANDING:

A young foreigner meets a Thai girl for lunch. She does the wai and he returns the gesture. To go back to his hotel he hails a taxi. The older driver, upon receiving a good tip, *wais* him, and drives off. The foreigner waves his hand to mean "never mind."

Some days later, the girl invites him to her house. An old man walks out and she introduces her father, whom he instantly recognises as none other than the taxi driver.

Now, should the westerner, say, a manager of some firm (status), recognising the tax-driver father (elder person), *wai* first? Or don't *wai* but mumble something in English as a detour? Or merely extend a hand out for a handshake? Do nothing to see what happens first?

Before he could sort himself out, a woman looking younger than he walks in and his girl friend introduces the woman as her step-mother. Should he *wai* this younger woman first or wait for her to do it first? An elderly woman now comes in and it turns out she is the chief servant. He becomes confused. *Wai* quickly?

Over to you.

Concerning.......

RELIGION

The areas that can possibly affect visitors where unintentional annoyances could be caused are:

The temple building

The temple ground

Monks and Nuns

Images

Statue sites

Books

Personal attire

Let's start from the bottom. It looks strange how something 'personal' in clothing can cause offense religiously in Thailand.

With due respects to all foreigners regardless of country of origin, the following observances are strongly solicited in the 'personal' sector.

PERSONAL

DO CHANGE CLOTHES

If you are already dressed for the beach, in very loose blouse or semi see-through top or short shorts -this includes the men as well- and then decide to visit a temple before the sea, well, change into 'acceptable' clothing first. If this is too bothersome, **don't go at all.** Decent attire is a must to the vicinity of **any** temple, including its compound. No exception.

We provide below some dos & don'ts on a very popular temple (*wat* in Thai) in Bangkok, which, with some 400 temples, should offer the religion-fascinated tourist enough ground for some self discovery of historical facts.

WAT PHRA KAEW (Temple of the Emerald Buddha):
Not permissible clothing: apart from what has

been mentioned above, also: knee-torn jeans, jeans shorts with frills, jogging trousers, sleeveless blouses or tops and open-feet sandals (flip flops). Visitors may change to proper top and/or bottom at the wat, which has these, without any charge. It means wearing some clothing that others have used before you came along. To be or not to see is entirely up to the visitor.

Please leave your document for quarantee.

PASSPORT
CREDIT CARD
BANK CARD
DRIVER'S LICENCE
IDENTIFICATION CARD
STUDENT'S CARD

FREE OF CHARGE

DO NOTE THAT visitors will also have to leave their passports at the clothes-changing area. The documents are in good hands as the staff are government servants, who will issue acknowledgement receipts and swap them back for the passports. Obviously, these receipts should not be lost.

DO NOTE ALSO that taking photos of the Emerald Buddha statue itself is not permitted.

BOOKS

DO NOT SIT / PLACE FEET / OBJECTS ON THEM

Often foreigners reading books on Buddhism casually discard them on benches in public places or on couches at home. Then something is placed over them or you sit on them like you do sometimes with other books or newspapers. It will offend a Thai to see a plate of fried rice or a glass of coke over the picture of a revered monk on the book cover.

Reverence for all things religious is very ingrained in the country. Accept this principle and many hours touring a temple and elsewhere can be happy times.

STATUE SITES

DO TREAT THEM WITH RESPECT

These are in street corners, at a building ground, in a Thai house where a special room might be solely devoted to statues, within a temple ground, on a mountain site along a highway or anywhere at a historic location. The respect extended is the same: consideration and homage.

One of the most popular statues in Bangkok is at the junction where the Grand Hyatt Erawan Hotel is located. Many devotees can be seen there, 365 days a year, praying for favours and offering gratitude for those granted. This is easily the most fascinating 'tourist' site for a religious ritual. Photography of the devotees, statue and dancers in classical costumes is permitted.

Anyone may buy a garland and/or joss sticks and place it together with the hundreds of others already there and who knows, this Erawan Statue may just grant the wildest wish that seemed impossible! Many beautiful stories abound about this statue but unfortunately there is no space to do it justice in this booklet. Suffice it to say that foreigners, if seeing it for the first time, should not mock or laugh at a statue with 'four' faces. It is one face, guarding the four points of the compass.

DO NOT VENTURE INTO A RELIGIOUS ROOM

Probably after sometime, many foreigners will come across in a friend's house an entire room or a good portion of it devoted to the Buddha. Here, tiers of steps have statues of all sizes and possibly in various postures such as sitting or standing.

One thing not to do is to venture into the room without permission, because your friend may have an envelope or two nearby a statue that he would not like to be seen by others. Also, Thais would approach this 'altar' in proper rituals of *wai* that a foreigner might not know how to do, like touching the forehead to the floor in a kneeling posture.

DO NOT MISTREAT AN OUTDOOR RELIC

At times, the more interested in ancient history might join a group outing that visits a statue still embedded to the ground, partly covered by grass with ants crawling over it. This could be in the middle of nowhere. Still, maintenance of proper respect is automatically expected. To be precise, it is *always* expected, regardless. It will simply not do, to sit on it (!) or position a foot somewhere and be photographed. Such things are never done by any local.

IMAGES

DO NOT THROW SMALL RELIGIOUS OBJECTS ABOUT

There are several forms, two being of human being: amulets of revered monks and mini statues of the Buddha. These are usually worn round the neck by a Thai. Then non-human figures are also worn. Whatever the form and however 'ridiculous' it might look to the new arrival or disbeliever, they should be accorded their dues: do not, for instance, at a shop or squatting in front of a sidewalk vendor, fling the object to a friend. Though done without malice but out of sheer laziness to walk over to give it to the friend to see, this action is sacrilegious to any Thai or anyone who is well cultured to respect religion, whichever that is.

EXPORTING STATUES

DO CERTIFY IF OFFICIAL APPROVAL IS REQUIRED

A religious statue is a revered symbol of the Buddha. Thus, regardless of the material, size, age or creation, it is expected to be respected all the time. This is unlike western thinking where so long as it is not blessed by a priest, the article is just an article and can be put in a pocket, pack with clothing or put on a stool. A misunderstanding can therefore arise in this direction. *All Buddhist religious articles should be respected* is how a Thai would view it.

Many visitors take a fancy to buying home statues for keepsakes, which is acceptable; nothing wrong in this but there are a few requirements.

First, strictly speaking, no religious article may be exported without the approval of the Fine Arts Department. This is to prevent indigenous work, rare specimens and national treasures and temple objects from disappearing from the country.

Where a visitor should like to export any Buddha statue, it is best the dealer be asked about exporting conditions, as he would be aware of them and would know how to go about it legally: filling in forms, getting the statues inspected, securing the approval stamp, etc.

If a statue is bought off a street vendor, the buyer should be prepared to answer Customs' questions and should expect the article to be confiscated.

MONKS AND NUNS

More likely, short-time visitors might not even see a white-robed, clean shaven head female religious person. Happily, there are less rules (for the stranger that is) governing the nuns than the saffron robed monks.

Whether the person in yellow robe is eighty years old or an eight-year old boy, Thais accord them proper respects, though obviously the small fellow gets less reverence.

The probable area of real contact with a monk, outside the temple area, could be in a public transportation system: the bus, boat or train.

WOMEN MUST NEVER TOUCH A MONK OR HIS ROBE

Rule number one: women should never, repeat never, touch a monk. Even in a train, bus or plane: women cannot sit next to the man in yellow. No exception.

How should a woman give something to a monk then? Upon indication that the monk is to receive anything from a woman, he will extend part of his robe onto the table or floor for the object to be placed on; it could just be a toothpick! Then, he withdraws the cloth and takes it. Alternatively, a lady could give it to a third person, a male, to pass it on.

DO TRY TO SIT LOWER THAN A MONK

Rule number two: no one should sit with his/her head higher than the monk's. That's why in temples, monks sit on a platform.

At home, where a platform might not be convenient, monks sit on a straw mat while the house people sit directly on the floor. The monks are therefore 'higher up' though a six-foot man will tower over a five-foot tall monk when both are facing each other sitting down. No matter, the monk is still elevated by the thickness of the mat. This is merely symbolic to practice a principle.

DO *WAI* THE MAN IN SAFFRON ROBE

Rule number three: one should always *wai* a monk when he comes face-to-face for a 'chit chat.' The monk will never wai back. At most, he will smile. Even if he appears to ignore the *wai,* remember that he cannot return the same gesture. But that does not mean he does not appreciate your respects for him.

Monks have hundreds of rules to observe; this is one of them, not 'wai-ing' back.

IN THE TEMPLE GROUND

DO PRACTISE PROPER BEHAVIOUR

Here, posing "disrespectfully" next to a *bo* tree or any statue or relic for photographs is frowned upon. Any tree for that matter with strips of coloured lace cloth tied round it should not be debased by a woman in an alluring pose even if she should be a beauty queen, film star or model. Respect for religion knows no social status nor colour of skin. It's like no one is above the law concept.

Temple ground is often kept clean. It serves as a place for strolling and even meditation by monks and accord some open air area where fellow monks could congregate for some discussion. There may be chairs, fountains, miniature gardens, steps,

whatever but the fact remains that it is 'holy' ground. These surroundings can be truly serene and beautiful on a mountain or at a beach.

DO NOT DISPLAY SEXUAL AFFECTIONS

Visitors should help to keep the place 'religious' by not holding hands or kissing even if they are newly weds because such sights can cause discomfort if seen by a monk accidentally on a stroll.

By and large, Asians do not display physical closeness or body contact to loved ones in public places and good foreigners are expected to follow suit.

THE TEMPLE BUILDING

Surprisingly, there is only one other rule to remember aside from the need to be decently attired. This is the footwear.

DO REMOVE FOOTWEAR BEFORE ENTERING MAIN AREAS

The shoes must be removed before entering certain sections, especially the main hall. Happily, in the more popular tourist-visited temples, there are signs, albeit these could be more polite (!), requesting removal of footwear. If there were to be none and a visitor is all alone, the thumb rule is to see if there is an altar with a Buddha statue. If there is the shoes **must** come off.

An acceptable question perhaps is: why must shoes be removed? This implies also, why must monks go about bare footed sometimes? If leather shoes/boots are objectionable, what's wrong with a pair of 'Japanese' slippers?

The answer lies in the fact that when a monk or layman approaches a Buddha image or in exercising some religious rite in the Buddha's name, the person should lower himself to the lowest. Thus, barefoot contact with the ground is the ultimate anyone can lower himself to for the Buddha. Wearing sandwich-thin slippers still make the wearer elevated by that margin. That's why at times monks do wear shoes, when they are 'off duty.' But for him to approach a Buddha image with his feet not touching the ground is unthinkable. For many Westerners where shoes are second nature, the dirty and black feet of monks walking about while on their rounds for alms in the early morning, must be quite an unhygienic sight. But, knowing the real reason, one must give credit to this practice of total humility for the Buddha.

ASKING PERMISSION FOR PHOTOGRAPHY

Most temples tolerate photography but it is best if permission is sought first if a monk is seen to be around, especially if a praying session were to be in progress.

DO TUCK THE FEET AWAY

If an occasion arises where sitting down is required, be sure to remember to tuck the feet away from a person or Buddha image. A monk will sit on a platform during consultation but if there is no raised seat for him and he sits on the floor then you may sit on the floor too with the feet tucked away from view.

BUDDHISM BACKGROUND

*T*he state official religion is Theravada or Hinayana Buddhism and about ninety percent, if not more, of the population are Buddhists. Buddhism, of course, comes from its founder, Gautama Buddha (563-483 B.C.) of Nepal in India.

It is believed by some academics that Buddhism came to Thailand during King Asoka's time, 269-237 B.C. brought by Indian merchants and emigrants and particularly by two monks, Phra Sona and Phra Uttara. Hinduism came as well and there is evidence of devotions to the Indian gods Vishnu and Siva, such as those stone depictions at temples in Phimai and Lopburi. From around 700 A.D. Mahayana Buddhism was introduced to Thailand but some three hundred years later Hinayana Buddhism was re-introduced by Burma.

Hinayana is the orthodox, based on Pali scripture while Mahayana is an enlargement of the original doctrine and based on the Sanskrit scripture but translated from the Pali text.

The following account of some basic information on Buddhism is taken from brochures published by the Tourism Authority of Thailand.

THERE ARE FOUR NOBLE TRUTHS:

1. The Noble Truth of Suffering,

namely, of birth (rebirth), disease, old age, death, sorrow, lamentation, pain, grief, despair; association with objects we dislike, separation from objects we love. Not to obtain what one desires causes suffering. There are many happy hours and pleasure in a man's lifetime but they are impermanent, lasting for a short time and vanish into nothing, by the law of nature. In other words,...

DO KNOW THAT Buddhism says our existence is but suffering caused by desires.

2. The Noble Truth of the Cause of Suffering,

The Threefold Craving: Sensual craving; craving for existence and craving for wealth and power. There is also a further six-fold craving: the eye craves for forms, the ear for sounds, the nose for smells, the tongue for taste, the body for objects and the mind for dreams.

DO SEE THAT these cravings and ignorance of the law of nature are the conditions of the origin of individual sufferings.

3. **The Noble Truth of the Cessation of Suffering.**The condition of the cessation of suffering is the complete fading away and extinction of this three-fold craving, forsaking it and giving it up, the liberation and detachment from it.

DO NOTE THAT when the mind has given up all these three-fold and further six-fold craving, realisation of the Extinction of Cravings or *Nibbana,* or *Nirvana* in Sanskrit, is then possible. This is the ultimate desire of Hinayana Buddhism: the cessation of desires, meaning the end therefore of all suffering or *dukkha.*

4. **The Noble Truth of the Path leading to the Cessation of Suffering.** This is the Noble Eightfold Path, also called The Middle Path because it avoids the two extremes of sensual pleasure and self-mortification. These are:

1. Right Knowledge: intellectual grasp of the Teaching of Buddhism (or *Dhamma*), the Four Noble Truths and the Law of Karma.

2. Right Intention: elimination of all ambitions, revenge, hatred, greed, lust and violence.

3. Right Speech: stamping out all lies, controlling words, being courteous, truthful, letting no evil words escape from the lips; being compassionate and full of sympathy, with a heart full of loving kindness and free from secret malice.

4. Right Action: meaning the avoidance of destruction of any living being, of taking what has not been given, indulging in sensuality, slander, intoxicating liqour or drugs.

5. Right Livelihood: that is, pursuing a trade or occupation compatible with the above precepts.

6. Right Effort: preventing new evil entering one's mind, removing all evil already there. To develop such good in one's mind and maintaining this goodness.

7. Right Attentiveness: This is the continual recollection of all phenonmena about bodily structure, all parts of the human body, all states of health, all impurity and purity of mind, contemplation of various states of

mind and all kinds of tempera-
ments.

8. Right Concentration: which is the
threshold of Nibbana and consists
of the Four Great Efforts, namely,
To avoid and To overcome evil
states of mind, To develop and To
maintain good state of mind. The
purpose of attaining Right
Concentration is to develop the
eye of wisdom.

Due to strong religious influence, the
present Thai calendar has been historically
reckoned with Buddha's death, namely,
at 543 B.C. Thus, to convert Thai year into
the western year, say, 1995, we add 543,
giving us 2538, a figure used by locals.

Buddhism is so strongly ingrained that
every male reaching 20 years of age strives
to enter the monkhood at least once, for
three months at least, before his death.
But this period is adjustable today for
economic reasons. Any king of Thailand
must also be a Buddhist and should enter
monkhood for a period accordingly. Thus
the present king, His Majesty King
Bhumibol became a monk without special
privileges in 1956. So too did His Majesty's
only son, H.R.H. Crown Prince
Vajiralongkorn who entered the monastery
in 1978.

Information Sources

Buddhism, like all religions, is a complex subject and in Thailand, one could, luckily, gain more in-depth knowledge from various sources and meditation centres in Bangkok. Try:

1.**Wat Maha That**

Tha Prachan (next to old Grand Palace) Bangkok.
Tel: 222-4981 [Section 5, Secretary].

English explanation is possible in this meditation centre although the session is done in Thai.

2. **The Young Buddhist Association of Thailand**

58/8 Petchkasem Road Soi 54, Pasricharoen, Bangkok.
Tel: 511 0439; 5113549.

This meditation or *vipassana* centre is an ideal place for anyone as there are teachers who speak in English. Do check up on the kind of food and accommodation that would be available.

3. **The World Fellowship of Buddhists**
   33 Sukhumvit Road. Tel: 251-1188-90.

   The building is just after Soi 1 of Sukhumvit Road. On Wednesday evenings a meditation session in English is conducted. It also has good informative material on meditation centres in Thailand. The office opens 9.30 am to 4.30pm, Mon-Fri.

4. **Buddhist Association of Thailand**
   41 Phra Athit Road. Tel: 281-9563.

   This was formed in 1934 but it was not until 1969 that it was decided that the HQ and its Secretariate would be located in Bangkok permanently, as its members attended meetings in Japan, Burma and Nepal.

5. New Age Shop
   10/2 Sukhumvit Soi 33
   Bangkok. Tel: 260 9202; 259 7588.

SOME POPULAR MEDITATION CENTRES (M.C.)

As many foreigners are interested in experiencing a meditation session, the following centres could help.

DO CONTACT THEM for any change in or new information. Most would have a couple of monks who either hold a class in English or would translate Thai into English. Accommodation is usually dormitory and limited to a few people.

Chonburi: Wiwek Asom Vipassana M.C. Tambon Ban Suan, Amphoe Muang. Tel: 38-283766
English translation available.

Pathumthani: Wat Phra Dhammakaya Klong 3, Khlong Luang, Pathumthani,12120. Tel: 02-5169003/9.
Daily Dhamma sessions and open discussions.

Surat Thani: Wat Kow Tham International M.C. Koh Pha-Ngan, Surat Thani, 84280. There are foreign monks in resident. Advance *confirmation is necessary for participation.*

Ubon Ratchathani: Wat Pah Nanachat Ban Bung Wai, Amphoe Warin, Ubon Ratchathani, 34310.

MOSQUES

Particularly in the South, Islam has a popular following. If going into one is intended, the following guidelines should be noted:

DO PUT ON some kind of hat if you are a male. It will be noticed Muslims men either have a white cap to show they have been to Mecca the Holy City or else a piece of cloth is wrapped around like a turban. Many use the *songkok* headgear.

DO BE ALMOST FULLY covered up if you are a female, preferably with a scarf over the hair.

DO REMOVE all footwear before entering the mosque proper.

DO NOT go in if there is a religious gathering, unless you are a Muslim. Even then, you should find out what the gathering is about.

DO SECURE SOME approval, if possible, for photography; otherwise stick to the outside scenery.

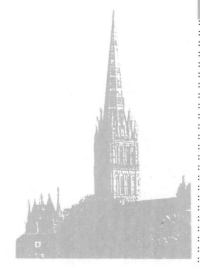

CHURCHES

This shouldn't be a problem, except one:

DO CHECK up to ascertain whether a service is in English or in Thai. Most hotel counters have no inkling of whether a mass is in English or Thai and you could be speeding to attend mass to find that you won't understand a word.

DO REMEMBER THAT as Thailand is basically a very staunch Buddhist country, Christmas is not celebrated widely, although all department stores and consumer goods shops doll up their premises. As such, X'mas presents are not expected. The attractive decorations, apart from hotels, are meant to usher in the new year. Hardly anyone says "Merry Christmas" to you on December 25.

Interesting notes on.....

THE MONARCHY

The Royal Family, by tradition of reverence and by love of all Thai people, commands a deep and genuine respect from young and old across the country.

Somehow, this Kingdom has been blessed with many benevolent monarchs who ruled with caring love for their people. Perhaps the best example to demonstrate the deep insight of Thailand's kings is the country's ability to prevent colonisation.

While neighbouring countries fell like dominoes, Thailand checkmated western powers. Leaders like Genghis Khan became known because of brutality; Thailand's rulers like King Rama V became loved because of brilliance. For those who are movie goers, we provide a short account of the present King so that when everyone rises when the Royal Anthem is played and His Majesty's picture is shown, you will have some idea about him.

DO TREAT all materials bearing any portrait of members of the Royal Family with due respect. This extends even to the currency which bears a portrait of His Majesty. In Thailand, it is not just paper money but it is also a *picture* of His Highness. Foreigners might find this hard to understand.

DO FIND OUT how to go about things if you have the happy occasion to attend a public event where a member of the Royal Family is present, e.g. our head should not be higher than the Royal Member's when he or she approaches our direction. At least we should keep the head slightly bowed when a Royal Member passes by.

DO NOT JOKE about the royal household even if you mean well. The Monarchy is one institution Thais do not joke about at all. Do it and the respect your friends have for you go down the drain. Worse, you could be charged with *lese majeste.*

DO NOT PASS any hurting comment even about past monarchs. Thais deeply respect their Kings and Queens even when they are no longer around.

SOME GREAT PAST KINGS

King Ramkhamhaeng 1279-1298 introduced the
Thai alphabet. This was during the Sukhothai
Period when culture was surging to a peak.
This king also introduced pottery works from
China and the country absorbed some elements
of administration and architecture from
Cambodia. At 19, he won a battle on elephant
back and his name means 'Rama the Brave.'
This king hung a bell at a gate so that anyone
wanting help could ring it and the king would
go to the person. A much quoted line of a
manuscript on stone done by the king himself
is: "There is fish in the water and rice in the
fields..."

King Narai, 1656-1688, sent the first Siamese delegation to the court of King Louis XIV of France after he had received letters from Pope Clement IX and the french king. It was the first ever overseas mission to a European country. (Is it any wonder that today, the post office parcel form is still printed in French and Thai? If you read neither language and want to send a parcel home, you have a problem).

King Rama I, 1782-1809, was the first king of the current Chakri dynasty. The king's name was Chao Phraya Chakri. He moved the capital from one bank of the Chao Phraya to the other side, founding present Bangkok. He moved the capital to avoid a Burmese attack. Thus the present Grand Palace was built, along with Wat Phra Kaeo (Temple of the Emerald Buddha). The king also restored Wat Po (Temple of the Reclining Buddha).

King Mongkut, Rama IV, 1851-1868, kept Siam from being colonised. He spoke many European languages and wrote in Latin as well. He tolerated Christian missionaries and was so good at astronomy that he predicted a comet's appearnace on the dot, beating a French team who was two seconds out! He corresponded with Queen Victoria who sent him presents that are in the museum today. Before he became king at 47 years old, he was a monk for 27 years. He was the monarch portrayed in 'The King and I.'

King Chulalongkorn, Rama V, 1869-1910, abolished slavery and greatly advanced public welfare and government system such as the introduction of the railway and telegraphs. He balanced various European powers to keep Thailand from being colonised.

THE PRESENT KING

It is difficult to do justice to the Present King in a few paragraphs like this because His Majesty, King Bhumibol Adulyadej, is easily the hardest Working Monarch today. Known for travelling all over the country to meet his subjects, His Majesty wears ordinary working clothes and treads through difficult terrain, usually with map and pen in hand.

The King is also a great music lover: he plays instruments and has composed many songs. He has donated his own money to help many projects in both the countryside and for Bangkok. There are so many areas where His Majesty takes a positive and effective interest that we cannot list them all here. The King is also an accomplished yachtsman, having taken part in many races.

One of the happiest days for Thais is His Majesty's birthday on December 5. Happiest because, for so many, it is their proudest day as it is officially 'Father's Day' as well. There is no Thai who does not genuinely love His Majesty whose principle concern is upgrading the quality of life of his subjects, particularly the poorer section in more remote regions.

The King was born in Cambridge, Massachusetts, USA, in 1927 and is currently the longest reigning monarch in the world.

For anyone who really wishes to have a good glimpse of His Majesty's early life and interests, there is a beautiful spacious public park on Srinahkrin Road. In this park there is a huge dome housing articles and photographs showing various aspects of His Majesty's life and work. In Thai, this park is known as *'Suan Luang Ro Kao'* (King Rama IX Park). This is on the same road as Bangkok's latest giant complex, the Seacon Square, but further out to another end.

PART 2

AROUND AND ABOUT

This ambiguous heading covers what you should do when you travel; be it on an overnight trip to up country, a short run to town or a quiet stroll in a park.

In the company of strangers you should always take precautions, regardless, if you do not want to lose your credit card, passport, cash or even an imitation Rolex or whatever you thought nobody would pinch. That's where you could just be wrong.

The following areas do not pertain to ingrained custom or rooted culture but, because they happen so frequently, a few Do's and a lot of Don'ts might prevent mishaps.

In any kind of......

ACCOMMODATION

Whether you are in a 5-Star or laying on your bedding under the stars, a few ideas on the country's environment should be noted.

SAFE KEEPING

DO AND DON'T (!) KEEP your valuables in a hotel safe deposit box. This is a tough one. Some safe deposit boxes are the most unsafe places for safe-keeping. Reason: Not all staff love you, foreigners and locals alike; they may be tempted to go for your credit cards. Entrust your life's possessions only to respectable hotels, which you have to decide which is respectable. Normally, 4-stars up are decent and honest, as are some family-type simple guest houses.

DON'T GIVE EVERYTHING in an envelope without itemising inside details. If you hand in travellers' cheques and foreign currency, have the receiver sign on your prepared piece of paper. YOU keep this paper; do not include it in the envelope. The duplicate key system is a farce sometimes, because someone in the hotel could have a triplicate! If you have no proof, you have no chance.

BILL DETAILS

DO ASK FOR a receipt if you pay for a room for more than a day. Some counter staff 'cannot find' any record of your payment and demand you settle for the day's rent, especially when you are checking out in a hurry. It is best to pay on a daily basis at cheaper types of accommodation. Remember that people who man the counter may be part-timers, work in shifts or could be off on your check-out day. You could be also offering yourself for a scam. Get a receipt!

DO CHECK DETAILS of your overseas calls even if you stay at 5-stars. So-called Executives Serviced Apartments are well known for careless(?) mixed ups. Check also to ensure that if the call was not made due to engaged line, you do not pay for it: the amount can lead to heated confrontation if you can only remember vaguely. If you should have a local female companion for the night, make sure you agree to her phoning her Monsieur Pierre in Paris for two hours; otherwise she will then phone her honey Tommy in Alaska also. Imagine your position if you stay in the same hotel for a week, have several ladies during this time and have a phone tab for something like 10,000 baht?

DO MAKE SURE your laundry is *your* laundry as it is returned. If possible, check it in front of the chambermaid or the man behind the counter. Be wary of the following assurring sign that is popular at some corner of a hotel: "Laundry - For Best Result: Drop your trousers here quickly." There are few DIY launderettes here. Cleaners charge not more than 12 baht per kilo at most places. Hotels have their own ideas.

NO LOCAL FEMALE GUEST

DO ADHERE TO prominent signs that say 'No Thai lady in room.' Two good reasons: One, to protect you from real harm like being drugged and robbed and two, for the hotel's image, to keep up its reputation. In between our first printing and this edition, the police have been more active in cleaning up vice-related activities of sex, drugs, theft and other crimes countrywide. Many incidents rose out of the casual one-night stand involving a Thai woman in the room even for just a few hours. The modus operandi is this: while you are in the toilet, she goes through as much of everything as possible. Or, when you are asleep, she does this. By the time you come out or wake up, you are alone, man!

BARE FACILITIES

DO BE PREPARED for down-to-earth facilities while travelling to remote places. The brochure will say 'serene beach' but it might not say 'no accommodation available.'

DO KNOW EXACTLY where you are going or doing, although you may have a map. Check up, before hand, on facilities before proceeding to the next remote 'place of sandy beach' or 'fresh mountain air.' It is surprising how even some seasoned travellers get caught due to negligence.

DO ACCEPT AN INVITATION to spend a night or two at a local's house upcountry if you feel you can trust your new-found friend. Exercise extreme self-protection and you should be o.k. Play by ear and go by common sense.

Single women should be very, very careful, even if there are two of you. Sometimes 'the more the merrier' when an ill-intentioned scheme lurks, like at a quiet beach house. Reporting to the local police brings little compensation usually. What **good** will that do you, really?

On going to...
THE CINEMA

Movie houses are no different here than in another country: they screen local as well as imported films. The only special feature is that just prior to the main film being shown, formal respect to the King is shown via a short screening of His Majesty's portrait and the playing of the Royal Anthem. This also applies to concerts and plays.

The inside atmosphere is also somewhat subdued and quiet comparatively.

DO RISE AT ROYAL PORTRAIT AND ANTHEM

Local patrons, regardless of age, would automatically stand up proudly as a mark of respect for him. It is worse than discourtesy for any foreigner not to follow suit: it visibly amounts to rejection of a very respected institution, the Monarchy and a downright insult to the King.

DON'T DO FUNNY THINGS AT THE BACK ROWS

In many countries, the idea of going to a movie sometimes is more to hold hands and maybe smooch all the way by sitting at the back row. This is not done in Thailand, at least not that commonly. It would be most healthy and in conformity with local public etiquette observations if gentlemen remain gentlemen at movie houses. Aside from distractions and setting a bad example for youngsters such scenes are embarrassing for local beholders.

DO KEEP FEET ON THE GROUND

One temptation for some people is to rest one foot or both feet up on the backrest of the seat in front when the seat is vacant. Granted that space can be tight for the long legged but give a thought: there are other very long-legged patrons too; well, how come they do not vulgarise themselves with their feet? The answer is that the feet, as indicated

in an earlier chapter, is considered to be the lowest part (meaning base) of the body and hence are viewed as improper for anywhere else but the ground.

DO LAUGH ALL YOU WANT

Some hilarious scene comes on. The natural thing to do is to laugh, and some people can really laugh. Should you laugh your loudest if that is normal for you?

Answer is, why not? Many Thais at Western films fail to catch on an implication either of action or via dialogue because Western culture and ways are alien to them. Sub-titles cannot convey the exact screen context, so they do not laugh at anything other than some outright comedy.

This is about the only area where you can let yourself go without fear of being impolite to your neighbour. If he can't appreciate something, that's his business!

DO NOTE THAT there are now several complexes that have a cluster of mini-theatres located usually at the topmost floor. You can go up to any counter and buy a ticket for any of the shows or cinema halls. Tickets are computerised and will indicate necessary information, just like an aircraft boarding pass. Simply sail through the correct door.

DO NOT FORGET to specify, at these mini-cinemas in shopping complexes, whether you want the sound track in English or Thai. The many TV screens overhead and numerous wall posters indicate relevant information.

DO REMEMBER THAT in all theatres smoking is not permitted.

If there is an...

EMERGENCY

Hopefully, no-one needs to use this section desparately. But,
should the need arises, also for some useful numbers, we hope
the information required is included here.

EMERGENCY

DO CALL THE following No Service Charge numbers accordingly:

POLICE	191; 123
HIGHWAY POLICE	193
TOURIST POLICE	1699
CRIME SUPPRESSION DIVISION	195
FIRE	199

Other important useful numbers are, for the Greater Bangkok Metropolitan Area (of Bangkok, Nonthaburi, Pathumthani, Thonburi and Samut Prakan):

Ambulance	
Police	25221715
Hospital	
Tourist Assistance Center	2815051; 2828129
Missing Persons Bureau	2823892 / 3
Immigration Department	2873101 / 10
Customs Department	2490431 / 40

If you are lost (!), cannot understand I-Saan or Southern Thai, or Chinese or Lao and have no friend and feel like giving up... DON'T! Call any of the Tourism Authority of Thailand (TAT) office or the Local Area Tourist Police and you will receive whatever assistance necessary.

The following (and all other) phone numbers are accurate as of printing time. It would be a good idea if the policeman you encounter cannot speak English - as is the case in most remote areas, - to call up the nearest TAT office before you dial your embassy, whose number it is suggested you take down before venturing all over the country alone.

TOURISM AUTHORITY OF THAILAND (TAT) OFFICE PHONE NUMBERS ARE:

	Place	Area Code	Tel: No (s)
Head Off.	Bangkok	02	2260060 / 72 / 85 / 98
Central	Kanchanaburi	034	511200
	Phra Nakhon Si Ayutthaya	035	246076 / 7
	Lop Buri	036	422768 / 9
Eastern Seaboard	Pattaya	038	428750; 427667
	Rayong	038	655420 / 1
	Cha-Am	032	471005 / 6
North	Chiang Mai	053	248604 / 7
	Chiang Rai	053	717433
	Phitsanulok	055	252742 / 3
Northeast	Nakhon Ratchasima (Korat)	044	213030; 213666
	Ubon Ratchathani	045	243770 / 1
	Khon Kaen	043	244498 / 9
	Nakhon Phanom	042	513490 / 1
	Udon Thani	042	241968
South	Hat Yai	074	243747; 238518; 231000
	Phuket	076	212213; 211036
	Surat Thani	077	288818 / 9; 281828
	Nakhon Si Thammarat	075	346515 / 6

EMERGENCY

TOURIST POLICE PHONE NUMBERS ARE:

Bangkok	1699 and (02) 225-7758
Pattaya	(038) 429-371
Chiang Mai	(053) 248-974
Hat Yai	(074) 246-733
Kanchanaburi	(034) 512-795
Phuket	(076) 212-213
Koh Samui	(077) 421-281

DO BE CAREFUL of snakes in damp, dark or thick grassy areas. If bitten, try to note the colours of the reptile. This will help a hospital doctor to prescribe the correct antidote. Poisonous fang marks are two punctures while non-poisonous bites are teeth marks formed like a horse-shoe shape.

DO REMEMBER THERE are hospitals with foreign doctors if so desired. At print time, some addresses are:

The Christian Hospital
124 Silom Road, Bangkok.
Tel: (02) 233-6981-9

Bangkok Adventist Hospital
430 Phitsanulok Road, Bangkok.
Tel: (02) 282-1100

The McCormick Hospital,
133, Kaew Nawarat Road, Chiang Mai.
Tel: (053) 241-010 / -107

For other medical information, a visitor can dial:

Medical Information Service,
Bangkok.
Tel: (02) 255-8222

94

SOME OTHER USEFUL PHONE NUMBERS

The following call services are free of charge:	
International Long Distance Service	100
Domestic Long Distance (+Malaysia and Vietiane)	101
Phone number assistance within Bangkok	13
Phone number assistance in provinces	183

RAILWAY STATIONS

Bangkok Hua Lampong: General	(02) 223-0341
Bangkok Hua Lampong: Information Unit	223-7010/20
Bangkok Hua Lampong: Advance Booking Office	223-3762, 224-7788

BUS STATIONS

	air-con coach	ordinary
Eastward Bound "Ekkamai"	(02) 391-2504, 391-8097	391-2504
Southward Journey "Sai Tai"	(02) 435-1199	434-5557/8
Northern Trip "Morchit"	(02) 272-0299, 272-5299	271-0101-5

AIRPORT

International Airport "Don Muang" (Thai Airways only)	535-1111	
Domestic Flight Information	535-2846/7	
Departure Details	535-1254,	535-1386
Arrival News	535-1301,	535-1310

TOURIST ATTRACTIONS AROUND BANGKOK

Grand Palace &	222-8181
Temple of the Emerald Buddha	ext 40
(Wat Phra Kaew)	224-3290
Temple of the Reclining Buddha	222-0933,
(Wat Pho)	225-3103
Marble Temple	281-2501
(Wat Benchamabophit)	
Snake Farm - Pasteur Institute	252-0161-4
Dusit Zoo	281-2000
National Museum	224-1396
National Arts Gallery	281-2224
National Theatre	224-1342
Shed of the Royal Barges	424-0004
Safari World	518-1000-19
Crocodile Farm	387-0020
Rose Garden Resort	253-0295-7

PUBLICATIONS

NATIONWIDE ENGLISH-LANGUAGE NEWSPAPERS

Currently there are two morning Dailies that are well distributed.

DO NOTE HOWEVER, in some wayout parts of faraway provinces. that only the previous day's edition is usually available, limitedly. It is thus quite mind-bogging in these 'off the beaten track areas' to hear over the air that so-and-so has died and then to read the next day that he is going to die! You can't help feeling that Mr Soso is not prepared to die.

The contact information of these two newspapers are:

The Bangkok Post, Bangkok Post Building 136 Na Ranong Road, Off Sunthorn Kosa Road, Klong Toey, Bangkok 10110. Tel: (02) 240-37700-79. Fax: Editorial: 240-3666

THE NATION, 44 Moo 10, Bangna-Trat Road K.M. 4.5, Bangna, Phra Khanong, Bangkok 10260. Fax: Editorial: 317-2071

MAGAZINES AND PERIODICALS

These are numerous and easily available but a good number are woman's magazines and mainly in Thai. The latest international names to hit the market are *Elle* for the fairer sex and *Penthouse* (Thai edition) with pin-up covered up for the other sex. Bi-monthlies or Fort-nightlies are in the vernacular.

MORE PHONE NUMBERS

DO CALL THEM up in the (02) Bangkok Area if need be.

S.O.S.	323-0640
The Samaritans of Bangkok	249-7530
Association of the Blind of Thailand	245-9846
Foreign Correspondents Club of Thailand	237-4764-5
Musical Artists Association of Thailand	587-4612
German Shepherd Dog Association of Thailand	279-3621
Overseas Missionary Fellowship	286-5085
Planned Parenthood Association of Thailand	579-0084-6
Press Association of Thailand	241-2064

Witnessing a......

FESTIVAL

Thailand, annually, probably has more festivals than her neighbours. Some are localised, others celebrated countrywide. Many festivals take on a carnival atmosphere where entertainment, exhibitions, display of produce and contests are not uncommon. A standard feature seems to be a beauty contest of local lasses.

One of the most interesting is the Songkran Festival, beginning on April 13 and lasts for three days officially. Here's where sometimes tempers (and also fists) flare up in all directions because of 'water-throwing.' Another colourful festival is Loy Krathong, held in mid-November on a variable date, amongst other equally splendorous celebrations.

SONGKRAN

DO UNDERSTAND that throwing water at anybody is an age-old happy event during Songkran. It is accepted; in fact expected. The other aspect of this festival is smearing the face with rice or tapioca powder.

DO NOT TURN violent if some cheeky lad were to try to smear your lady's friend's face. Granted you could be right for he is insistent but try to find a way out somehow without using the fist. This had happened and made local headlines which makes everything very sad. (Here's a bad suggestion: Get the powder off him and show you want to smear his face also. Then give him the hardest rub you can. The white powder will prevent any redness from showing. Teach him a lesson, but don't hit him?)

DO NOTE THAT public buses are the most sought after targets. Apart from huge buckets of water, the more naughty ones resort to rubber hoses and literally splash the whole busload. Buses are "ambushed" at strategic spots like traffic lights.

SIGNIFICANCE: Marks the beginning of a new year for Thais. The word 'Song-kran' in Sanskrit means the beginning of a new solar year. This is on April 13 and the celebration lasts for from three days to a week in some places. It is the fifth Thai lunar month, marking the assumed entry of the Sun into Aries. The ceremony celebrates the transference of the sun, Surya, to the New Cycle.

Buddhists will clean all Buddha images with scented water; monks and family elders are sought out and lustral water poured over their hands to ask for their blessings for happiness and good fortune. Still practised in some parts of the kingdom is the unique custom of releasing live birds, fish and where available, tortoises, to their freedom. (This is a dying practice in the face of increasing awareness of environmental preservation as the action encourages more birds and fish to be caught only to die and not to be released). In olden days, farmers would catch baby fish from ponds that began to dry up after the rainy season. The fish are bred until Songkran when they are released into canals. The farmers believe they would gain merit through this good deed while ensuring there is fish in the water.

Chiang Mai is where the celebration is merriest and many visitors go there just for its fun.

DO JOIN IN in the water-throwing. Throw water, iced it first if you want, and whack it at that policeman you don't like. He cannot arrest you during the official festive period.

Want to *try?*

LOY KRATHONG

DO TAKE PART in lighting a candle and letting it float down a stream or canal or in a hotel pool or special place set up specifically. It has no religious connotation but originated from people wanting to send their love to sweethearts and loved ones faraway. During this time, at the end of October or beginning of November, plastic foam 'krathongs' can be seen on sale almost everywhere. These are round, with flowers and a candle in the middle of the 'boat.'

SIGNIFICANCE : 'Loy' means to float; 'krathong' is a leaf cup, usually of banana leaf deftly folded into a container looking like a cup. A candle is positioned onto this cup and the boat-looking vessel is released into a river as an offering sacrificed to Mae Khongha, the Mother of Waters. There are several versions for the festival which is beyond the scope of this book to describe in length, but the accent was to let the little krathong carry your thoughts and love to those who are far away from you. Romantic, for sure.

When the full moon begins to rise in the evening, people carry their krathongs to the river or lake to let these lighted 'ships' float away. In today's world, the floating life of some of these beautiful krathongs is short, as children scramble to search for coins that are often placed on the floats.

Hours of painstaking work dommed within minutes, for some, seconds. But those that float on, against a usually dark but silvery water surface, is something to behold - as there may be dozen, scores or hundreds of them.

ROYAL PLOUGHING CEREMONY

DO DROP BY to Sanam Luang, the big field next to the Grand Palace in Bangkok, if you are in town, during the sixth lunar month, i.e. second week or so of May. This is a very important event to every farmer, meaning about 80% of the population, as it signals the auspicious beginning to start ploughing for the new rice crop. His Majesty the King starts the ceremony off by appointing a Lord of the Festival, a *phya rack nah* as his representative to officiate the rites.

DO TAG YOUR camera along to film the colourful procession of red and gold sacred plough, pulled by garlanded bulls with celebrants costumed in green or red. Film the scramble of hundreds of farmers as they 'fight' to gather a few grains of the ceremonial rice on the field. Farmers come from distant farm lands to take home this rice - even one grain will make a farmer happy,- to mix with their new seedlings to ensure a bountiful crop.

SIGNIFICANCE: The indication of a good date to start ploughing is important and with the King participating, its importance is enhanced greatly. Historically, the ruler has always taken part in this ceremony. King Rama V wrote that the origin could be traced back 2500 years ago, to the Lord Buddha's time!

TROOPING OF THE COLOURS

DO SEE THIS colourful event if you are in town around December 3. Their Majesties the King and Queen preside over the occasion in the Royal Plaza near the King Chulalongkorn statue in Bangkok.

There is much pomp as smartly dressed Royal Guards swear allegiance to the King and march past members of the Royal Family to mark the King's birthday on December 5.

THEIR MAJESTIES' BIRTHDAY CELEBRATIONS:

THE QUEEN'S ON AUGUST 12; THE KING'S ON DECEMBER 5.

Throughout Thailand, the Thai Flag flutters atop many buildings and even on bus and tuk tuk windows. Such is the deep reverence extended by all Thais for the King and Queen on these two dates. Government and public buildings are splendidly adorned with buntings, portraits, flowering plants, banners and fairy lights, transforming every city and town into a fairy land atmosphere.

The vicinity along Rajdamnern Avenue near the Royal Plaza in Bangkok is traditionally the best lighted and decorated area, albeit 'compitition' from private enterprises all over town. In the Provinces, prominent government buildings and main roads would be similarly donned up.

DO SEIZE THIS opportunity for night photography for those visitors who are shutter bugs. As these are nationwide holidays, it is also a good time for a day out.

SURIN ELEPHANT ROUND-UP

DO RESERVE ACCOMMODATION well in advance if you are around the festival time in November, the actual date varies. So many past visitors were disappointed when they arrived at Surin town, wasting time and effort. Around 100 elephants will demonstrate their skills and illustrate their role in history when Siamese kings used them as war machines.

DO TAKE A ride on an elephant's back if you have never been on one.

OTHERS

DO CHECK UP ON the many other festivals that are held every month in one province or other. Leading hotel lobbies may have complimentary weekly periodicals or some write ups from brochures.

DO BE AWARE where a festival involves some animals like monkeys or pigs, buffalo, elephants and other creatures, the animals can turn violent if frightened suddenly. They are trained but they can also be panicky.

DO LOOK OUT FOR the speciality in a festival. It could be a fruit or a piece of handicraft. Try them out lest you miss something that might not come your way again until the next year.

DO SEE IF any of the following appeals to your taste and then check up for changes and more details. The Tourism Authority of Thailand (T.A.T.) will oblige. There are many other fairs and festivals apart from these highlights.

event	place	month
Umbrella Fair	Chiang Mai	January
Arts & Crafts Fair	Ayutthaya	February
Dragon & Lion Parade	Nakhon Sawan	February
Flower Float Festival	Chiang Mai	February
Barred Dove Festival	Yala	March
Kite Flying International	Bangkok	March
Pattaya Festival	Pattaya City	April
Lychee Fair (Lychee is a sweet fruit)	Chiang Rai	May
Rocket Festival	Yasothon	May
Phi Ta Khon Festival ('phi' is ghost in Thai)	Loei	July
Candle Parade	Ubon Ratchathani	July
Longan Fair (Longan is a sweet fruit)	Lamphun	August
Langsat Fair (Langsat is a sweet fruit)	Uttaradit	September
Boat Race	Phichit	September
Boat Race	Phitsanulok	September
Boat Race	Nan	October
Vegetarian Festival	Phuket	October
Illuminated Boat Procession	Nakhon Phanom	October
Buffalo Race	Chon Buri	October
Banquet for Monkeys	Lop Buri	November
King's Cup Sailing Regatta	Phuket	December
I-Saan Kite Festival	Buri Ram	December

Going along to your....

FRIEND'S HOUSE

To be invited to spend a night at a Thai friend's house is not usual. Thais much prefer a slow and steady progress to a relationship. To bring along an opposite sex friend constitutes a violation of an invitation. To bring along another friend of the same sex can make your guest unhappy. The Thai invited you, not your friend.

DO NOT WALK INTO THE HOUSE WITH FOOTWEAR ON

Even if your shoes are brand new, of genuine leather, from Italy and has cost a fortune, leave them where they should be left. You either respect your friend or your shoes! Remove them, at least at the main doorway even if your friend says it's all right. It's *not* all right. All Asian countries observe this discipline and Thailand is more particular than elsewhere.

If there is a hole in one or both socks, remove the socks. It's better to be barefoot like your host than having a toe sticking out like a tortoise head, don't you agree?

The need for shoe removal stems from the fact that Asians sit, sleep and for rural Thais, even eat on the floor. Without shoes no dust, mud and dung would be brought in. There is no religious significance; it's just a matter of hygiene.

DO NOT STEP ON THE DOOR THRESHOLD

This main doorway, the threshold, has certain significance in Thai culture. Do not step on it if you linger at the door. **Do not step on it at all but over it when getting in and out of all doors.**

DO SIT IN ONE PLACE INDICATED BY YOUR FRIEND

You cannot simply sit anywhere you like, once inside the house. If you are not directed, ask where may you sit and consider that your sitting kingdom. Return to it always.

Many houses in the
tables. The folks sit on the floor, with the men
crossing their legs one on top of the other and the
ladies tucking them gracefully to one side. On first
go, many Caucasians find these postures killing and
even impossible.

What should one do in such a case? Apologise;
and a stool or something to prop up your posterior
will come up.

DO NOT WALK INTO THE KITCHEN/ BATHROOM

You cannot simply walk
into a kitchen or
bathroom to get yourself
a drink or release some. The
correct thing to do is to get
permission first and then go.
At any rate, some drink for
refreshment, usually plain
water, will be offered to you
before long.

To go to the loo, simply
ask and you will be directed.
You cannot just head
automatically for the only
other door in the room. This
may be the closet! The
bathroom may be outside and
behind the house.

DO *WAI* AT AN ELDERLY PERSON

When an elder appears, never mind who, the
most polite etiquette is to engineer a *wai* before
this person beats you to it. (He/she would not

normally initiate it). But make sure you are not *wai-ing* the servant!

What to do then? Best thing is to immediately ask your friend, "Is this your parent?" If he is a good servant, you would be *wai-ed* first or, if he/she is bringing drinks, you can know from her manner of approach: head slightly bowed, eyes to the floor. When she serves drinks, notice how she does it -it makes you feel like you're a king or queen.

The two most important persons in the household are your host's father and mother. The appropriate greeting/calling terms are *Khun Phor* for the father and *Khun Mae* for the lady. You are actually calling them "dad" and "mum" like your host. This is the warmest and most polite address you can give the old folks. In Western culture, it will look ridiculously out of place to call a friend's father 'dad.' (What would mom think?!!). To everyone else who appears older than you, a plain *Sawatdee krup* is sufficient with a proper *wai* on first contact.

ACCEPT THINGS WITH YOUR RIGHT HAND

I n Asia, the left hand is used to wash the posterior and hence is 'less clean.' In fact, it would be impolite to offer or accept anything with the left hand, even if you are left-handed. This is not easy to remember for the left-handed because of reflex action, but do *try?* We had already mentioned this point earlier on but its importance justifies a repetition.

NEVER SLEEP (OR WALK ABOUT) IN YOUR UNDERWEAR

S leeping time is sleeping time anywhere but, in a Thai house, no one would sleep in the underwear when a guest is around though the weather may be unbearably hot.

The visitor must never sleep in undies even among the same sex or a room was specially given. The reason is respect for others in the house, decency in sleeping and dignity to oneself. It is hard to imagine a Thai/Asian sleeping in the raw in his own room.

NO NEED TO SAY 'GOODNIGHT'

Thais do not say 'good night' (nor 'good morning'). When it's time to sleep, just smile and follow your friend. You could of course say 'goodnight' but you will most probably be stared at. With modern Thais who had cultivated some western culture, not to say so would be quite unexpected! It's yes and no depending on the situation.

BRINGING A FRIEND ALONG

A problem might arise when you want to bring an uninvited friend along. If it is the same sex, it might place a burden on your friend as it is you only who are wanted. If the uninvited friend is the opposite sex, some real problems will arise.

The difference lies in the fact that in western society, a host will allow a guest to sleep on the couch or anywhere the guest indicates. In Thai society, the guest is a VIP and the best the family can give will go to the guest. A father and mother might give up their room for their son and his guest, while they sleep elsewhere. Now, how can the son sleep with a male guest who has a female companion? In Thai society, there is no way these three can sleep in the same room in a respectable house. If your host gives up his room for you and your sweetheart, he might have to sleep somewhere uncomfortable. You wouldn't want that, would you? Also you will most certainly not be welcomed to sleep there again.

Before trying to bring a friend where overnight stay is intended, it is best to clear with your host first. If your host does not know your friend and you have never seen your friend's place, drop the idea of going at all. This would be better than to tag the other person along unannounced.

DO NOT EXPECT BREAKFAST

In the morning, do not expect breakfast in the western sense. There will most likely be no coffee, toast or anything until maybe around 10am or later, when the meal could be rice. Do not ask "May I have some coffee?" because by and large Thais do not drink coffee in the morning nor tea in the afternoon; they may have neither in the house or they may have both, depending on whether your friend is a typical rural person or a 'modern' man living western-style in large cities.

If there is a coffee stall nearby, you could be direct, excuse yourself and hop over there for your indulgence. No one might accompany you and you risk insulting your local innocent host later. You will have to make up your mind which is more needed at that moment. (Coffee addicts will have no problem, obviously!).

"HERE ARE SOME APPLES"

I t is *not* necessary nor expected but it would be nice not to go to a friend's house "empty handed." Locals of Chinese origin among themselves usually cart some edibles along for the children, old folks or everybody. Ethnic Chinese practise this across the globe by bringing along some fruits and confectioneries, usually fruits.

Alternatively, you will be loved for giving some of these token goodies that you have bought from the local grocery shop just prior to your departure. The practice is, "It's the thought that counts."

WEAR ANYTHING OTHER THAN FULL BLACK

D o not wear full black at all while going to or in a friend's house. This is the colour of mourning. None of your guest will tell you but they will be tolerating in silence and sadness your lack of decency to the household.

SOME USEFUL THAI PHRASES

I am tired	*phom/chan neuai*	ผม/ฉันเหนื่อย
I am sleepy	*phom/chan nguang-nonn*	ผม/ฉัน งวงนอน
Where are you going?	*khun chah pai nai*	คุณจะ ไปไหน
The food was delicious	*aharn a-roi maak*	อาหารอร่อยมาก
How many rooms are there?	*thang-mod mi ki hong*	ทั้งหมดมี กี่ห้อง
Someone is knocking at the door	*mi khon khaw pratou*	มีคนเคาะ ประตู
My mother is not well	*mae phom mai sabaai*	แม่ผม ไม่สบาย
I don't speak Thai well	*phom phoud Thai mai keng*	ผมพูด ไทยไม่เก่ง
Do you have any more?	*mi ik mai*	มีอีกไหม
May I sit here?	*nang thi-ni dai mai*	นั่งที่นี่ ได้ไหม
It's not very far	*mai klai thao rai*	ไม่ไกลเท่าไหร่

FOR:	SAY:	THAI SCRIPT:
bedroom	hong nonn	ห้องนอน
clean	sa-aat	สะอาด
electricity	fai fah	ไฟฟ้า
(there's) no electricity	mai mi fai fah	ไม่มีไฟฟ้า
there's an electric fan	mi phat lom	มีพัดลม
pillow for sleeping	mawn	หมอน
blanket	phaa hom	ผ้าห่ม
cabbage	kalam pi	กระหล่ำปลี
cucumber	taeng-kwa	แตงกวา
long (string) beans	tua fak-yao	ถั่วฝักยาว
banana	kluai	กล้วย
buffalo	kwai	ควาย
catfish	pla douk	ปลาดุ
squid	pla muek	ปลาหมึก
lemon grass	takrai	ตะไคร่
is it (=are you) cold	nao mai	หนาวไหม
the weather's fine today	wan-ni ahkat di	วันนี้อาการดี

In attending a.....

FUNERAL

Most Thais are traditionally Buddhists, hence the widespread number of temples. But some are Muslims while a handful are Christians, of various dominations.

Buddhists are cremated, but there is a period of lying in state at the temple before the actual cremation. This instance is when most foreigners are likely to encounter if they have Thai friends.

COMMON CEREMONIAL RITES

We provide a brief description of the major necessities and rites a Buddhist family has to perform when someone passes away. There are bound to be some variations because of expense and convenience for the family members. A wealthy family with a large group of members can have, for instance, musicians specifically skilled in rendering appropriate music every night for many nights while a very poor woman with three small children to support now might not even be able to pay for extra chair rental for guests.

The rich family can and will give every guest an expensive memento while the poor woman in our example cannot afford to give anything. Thus a guest may be treated to different versions of a cremation ceremony in the same temple on different occasions.

Perhaps a parallel with a Catholic church ceremony might help to put a few points across: imagine a Thai Buddhist who has never stepped into a church attending a Low Mass and then a Requiem High Mass celebrated by a bishop for the same dead person. Would he be confused? This is what we are trying to explain.

When a local passes away and the body is placed in a temple, this is what happened and will centrally happen:

The decorated huge coffin box contains an actual more simple and smaller box that houses the body. This outer coffin consists of removable parts lashed together. On top of this is placed a huge plastic bouquet; smaller similar bouquets belonging to the temple are placed in front, together with a photograph of the person.

Every evening, beginning around 7.00pm four monks will recite prayers, each holding up a huge fan that completely covers his face. On cremation day, just before 11.00am, nine monks will pray, have lunch provided by the family and then depart. Guests will then have catered lunch there as well. If the deceased is a man, the widow would be wearing a white top and a black bottom for this occasion. She would change back to total black for the cremation.

At 4.00pm (the time differs slightly, depending on when it is best for cremation), a monk will deliver a short sermon to the gathering. The outer box is removed and the actual coffin is shouldered onto a waiting carriage, in the shape of a golden boat.

A monk will lead the procession thrice round the temple ground. The monk holds a string which is passed onto the widow/widower, then the children who are all in front of the carriage. The string is tied to this carriage. This symbolic walk to send the deceased to his next home is joined by all guests.

Guests will now sit in a pavilion facing the crematorium, where all the wreaths and additional flowers would decorate steps and ground. These flowers are not burned with the body, but are simply thrown away later.

New saffron robes are usually donated by the family for the monks' nightly service. The widow, let us say it is a woman, is accompanied up the steps of the crematorium where the coffin is now placed inside yet another outer box, of a different design. The robe is placed before the coffin and one by one, - the widow may have to walk several times, - a monks goes up to the coffin, says his thanks and accepts the robe.

The actual coffin is removed and placed in the incinerator. Guests will approach the burning chamber and symbolically throw in a specially prepared 'lighter' consisting of paper/straw strips that will light easily. Each guest will put this lighted strip in the bottom of the furnace. A metal container will therefore be emitting a small flame that could block the actual coffin from view. The coffin is placed well inside the chamber and will not be really burning.

On descending the steps, guests may be given a small gift as a souvenir of thanks for their attendance.

The chamber is securely bolted and attendants will activate the cremation. At this point, guests may begin to go home. Some might stay until no more smoke emits from the crematorium tower. So ends a sad ceremony.

DO WEAR BLACK OR WHITE ATTIRE to a pre-cremation ritual at a temple. For men, a white shirt will be polite and ladies either a black top or a full white or black dress. It will be seen that many local women will put on something very sober: black or dark gray and white combination.

Nothing should be red, pink or orangey including shoes and handbag. Most ladies opt for a black top at least. Ladies do not wear gloves, veils or hats in this country.

DO PRESENT SOME MONETARY TOKEN to the bereaved in a white envelope. The amount is up to you and your closeness to your friend. You could also bring a wreath along.

Upon arrival at the temple, locals would light one joss stick, kneel before the coffin and say something silently. They then place the joss stick in the jar with other joss sticks, offer a *wai,* back away a couple of steps before standing up abruptly and walking away.

You could do the same thing if you wish. It is just a mark of respect and expression of sorrow for the deceased. You could wait and see someone doing it first and then follow suit if you have no qualms about holding the incense. If you don't, as Catholics are not supposed to, explain to your friend.

DO TRY TO SIT THROUGH at least one session of the monks' prayers. You don't need to clasp your hands in the *wai* position though. The monks will recite prayers lasting about two or three minutes, recess, continue, recess and continue again. The whole praying session will last around an hour. During the recess period, the monks will still be seated on a platform.

Each monk will hold up a big fan in front of him while chanting.

DO ACCEPT REFRESHMENTS that will be served to guests. They have no religious implications but are provided as many people will sit through the whole night. You don't have to keep vigil with your friend more than an evening unless you want to.

DO EXCUSE YOURSELF and go off anytime you want, but time your exit during one of the recesses for politeness sake.

DO TRY TO ATTEND THE CREMATION, at the same temple if it is convenient for you. This is because cremation may take place after a few days, or weeks, months or 100 days. Sometimes it takes place a year later. Cremation is normally held in the afternoon, between 4.00pm till 5.00pm or before the sun sets at least.

This is, with pardon to ladies,...

MAINLY FOR MEN

This section may appear blunt and drastic to male readers but the intention is to be realistic.

There are many temptations for men in Thailand. Many men would already have wives and children. No man would want anything unfortunate to happen to him. This is only natural.

Yet, many leave the country worse off than when they came in. How come? Carelessness or plain foolhardiness? The following guidelines could be helpful.

Please read on, men!

DO NOT GET stone drunk alone in public places. If a man must get done (for whatever reason), do it in the hotel/apartment room, alone or with established friends only. Unfortunately, there are long-time resident foreigners who will 'do a new foreigner in' given the chance. **Sometimes a fellow foreigner can be more dangerous than a naughty local.**

Caucasians have committed suicide, ended up as beggars, gone missing, deported home or became amnestic jay walkers because of other Caucasians, some of whom are over-staying and intimidating new comers. There used to be 'farang' mafia-types operating (still are?) in Pattaya particularly. So:

DO BE SUSPICIOUS of your own kind, who may be here because he is running away from something or someone and is of despicable character. His aim: your money. He usually has a local for a side-kick and speaks good Thai since he would be a long-time fugitive here. Some got married to local girls merely for staying purposes to hunt around for victims.

DO NOT CARRY TOO MUCH CASH when visiting bars and such places. When a wallet is pulled out for bills to be paid, many eyes pop out to see what and how much is in your bag. If you are sure you are being followed, head for the police station, or report to hotel staff.

DO GO SLOW on local-name whiskeys. A couple of brands have imitation blends concocted in backyards and passed on to bars, restaurants and mini-stores.

DO BE ALERT of pickpockets all the time, especially if you appear tipsy. There used to be razor-sharp slickers who may still put their dexterous skills on your back pocket.

DO NOT TAKE ANY HOSTESS FOR GRANTED. Sometimes the more innocent she looks, the more dangerous she can become. Promises and pledges do not mean much to people in 'unbe-coming' professions. Remember too that girls seldom work alone when it comes to fleecing the stranger.

DO NOT ENGAGE IN UNPROTECTED SEX. Go
ahead if AIDS is yearned for as a bonus. What,
travel half way round the world and pay to get
AIDS? And (pardon!) die a slow death? The
presence of AIDS and incidence of spread is
serious and getting more serious in Chiang Mai
and Hat Yai as well. In fact, nowhere is safe as
prostitutes are always on the move.

DO NOT MAKE SERIOUS PROMISES you can't keep.
Some night women will cry their hearts out,
others may decide to take yours away, literally,
with some help from boy friends. Believe it,
your life may not be so valued if you make false

promises to lure girls to your intentions. Do not mistaken a sweet smile for a soft heart; many of the girls are forced by circumstances to work in bars and parlours for the money, not because they like you.

DO BE SUSPICIOUS of a local who says he likes you. This could be true but it might not last. The point is not to blindly believe what is said all the way. There is a Thai song with the following lyrics in English: "If no money, go home." There is a popular phrase, slung solely at the Caucasian: 'Cheap Charlie;' and there is a common remark one can hear quite openly: 'Stupid Farang.'

DO NOT UNWISELY follow a Thai woman, who could just be an office worker, whom you do not know *very* well, to her apartment. 'Your place or mind' can be the last place for you. You could be tricked into gambling, threatened until you sign something or simply blackmailed for you-know-what with his missus or worse, minor missus, translated as 'minor wife,' namely a mistress but openly and proudly kept as a secondary wife. This crazy acceptance allows a Thai man to have any number of wives without being crucified. For additional information, not that it will do any good but merely as a provocating thought: that is why there are so many ladies in the service - namely, flesh - trade; they get dumped by their husbands after they have given their worth. And they need to eat. And feed their youngsters, usually. As no Thai man will marry them, their next best bet is a foreigner who might provide the needs in a more beautiful country. To all of these dumped women, the grass is greener on the other wide side.

DO KEEP IN MIND that some *katoey* - men dressed in women's clothes - may have a champion-boxer's power when it comes to trading punches. Know also that these transvestites work in packs and they can run fast, once they discard their high heels.

DO TRY NOT to believe all sexy girls are female. Transvestites and transsexuals in Thailand are often outwardly and bodily more curvaceous and vivacious than natural girls. These groups can be extremely rude, dangerous and revengeful if a promise is broken, like you say "ok" after two beers. Then when you hear her manly tone or finally notice her cleverly hidden Adam's apple, or the scar where it had been shrunk surgically, you say "no." In a situation like this, it is best to pay up and end all conversation. Or get out of the bar or coffee-house.

DO NOT TAKE YOUR SKIN colour for granted. On the surface, the word 'farang' to you may seem like a sort of higher social status. Beneath it, if you do something wrong, you are in more serious trouble than back home, wherever that may be.

DO REPORT ALL CRIMES to the police if you were the victim or a witness. The Tourist Police generally speak understandable English and are trained to help the foreigner. If you care to, submit a copy of your report to the Tourism Authority. You could help to make the future a little better. If you care, that is.

DO BEHAVE WELL IN LADY SERVICE PLACES. It might be just a bar to you but shouting, losing temper and excessive noise lower respect *for* you. Keep your hands where they should be. Reason: Her husband/boy friend could be just opposite you! Also it is a disgusting sight to the local staff although a sex show could be in progress. There are differences.

MAINLY FOR MEN

DO BE AWARE of TOUTS, hustlers and all sorts of shady characters, especially if you are alone and **are about to leave anywhere.** Remember that you are being sized up by everybody the moment you walk into a bar/massage parlour for the first time. Fun places can turn out to be disastrous areas to kill time.

DO NOTE THAT IN SOME UPSTAIRS BARS in Patpong in Bangkok and elsewhere there can be a hidden charge to the drinks price. This amount can be very hefty. You take two beers, which should not be more than 150 baht at the present price, but your bill may show 7,000 baht. It's a rip off. Insist on calling the Tourist Police, not the ordinary cops as some of them are on the take.

DO NOT ABUSE LITTLE CHILDREN. You can help this country by rejecting every aspect of talk on child sex. Many children are SOLD by their parents to buyers for sex trade purposes. The youngsters, many have never been out of their calm village till then, are 'broken in' in ways that are sickening. If you see just *one* case on how it is done, you will never touch a child again. But do we have to witness something horrifying before we can be compassionate?

DO NOT BE ASHAMED if you are gay. So far, Thailand makes no distinction of such social fraternity. There are gay bars for anyone to partronise in major tourist areas.

DO KEEP YOUR three-piece suit in the hotel when you hit the shadier entertainment places at night. You are otherwise telling the management, "Hey, look. I'm new and I have a lot of money. Come and fleece me." Besides, the weather outside and the heat (from the women) inside makes a loose, open-necked tropical shirt more suitable. Go short-sleeve, colourful (makes you look younger), soft; not a starched, white, stiff, cuff-linked shirt with a tie so tight it creates a treble layer neck. This latter mode of dress should be used if you visit those ultra-expensive 'member clubs' where there is valet care for your SSS555000 Merz.

DO KNOW 'MEMBER CLUBS' in Bangkok also admit complete strangers on the spot for a 'small'(depending on one's idea of "small") entrance fee. Service is excellent, the ladies are excellent, the atmosphere is excellent. Expectedly, the bill is also excellent. You will need your credit card, preferably a gold one, to really have a jolly good time. The ladies should be tipped well if a second visit is intended. This is no place to bring the wife to.

DO NOT VISIT massage parlours alone for the first time if you cannot speak Thai or have not been here long enough to know that there is a double-standard in pricing for almost everything in the whole country. An honest-to-goodness one hour massage of 150baht may turn up to be 1500baht for the unwary first-timer.

Of course, if one is prepared for unwise involvement, one could do anything, in which case, this book is totally a waste of money and time.

Whenever & wherever at.....

PUBLIC PLACES

*About the only place where special care and respect
must be extended without exception is the temple and portraits
of the Royal Family; in other words, the religion and the
Monarchy, as separately discussed.*

*Regardless of where a touring visitor is, the following guidelines
should prove useful for a pleasant happening.*

DO MAINTAIN A PLEASANT VOICE

The Voice should always be soft and calm. Those who had witnessed a car accident would have noted that even in such a grave situation, there was none of the shouting, accusing, finger-pointing, wild gestures, name-calling and everything else that is so common in the supposedly more advanced West. Don't raise your voice anywhere or anytime at anyone even when you feel cheated and you need to demand an explanation. To do so is to 'lower yourself' and be seen as uncultured; perhaps a barbarian as one would say?

DO NOT LOSE YOUR TEMPER

Temper is related to the voice volume. To lose one's temper is even worse than raising the voice. Yelling away, cursing that fellow, wishing he would be re-incarnated as a rat/cat/dog/pig would not do you one bit of good in the eyes of a Thai. Come to think of it, what do you gain? In this country, you will be laughed at, which would irritate you even more and this will generate more laughter! If you don't want to 'make a fool of yourself' pardon the expression, hold your temper at all cost.

DO HAND THINGS OVER GRACEFULLY

The easiest way to pass a small object like a magazine or pen is to throw it to the other person. Don't. Not even across the table; not even sliding it across the table top. **Do not throw things to another person** even if you already know him for twenty years. It all has to do with respect for the other party. To throw something is like showing that you are unwilling to hand it over or you are angry or displeased with a situation. This therefore makes the receiving party awkward and anyway, a thrown thing often lands short or away from its target! So why throw really?

DO TRY AND SIT DECENTLY

In all Western countries, one can sit on the steps, floor or railing of some garden fence without drawing an eyelid from passers-by. One could even be engaged in a little light necking on a park bench in semi-lying down position and what have you. About the only person who would accost you is the chap in blue uniform with a truncheon and/or a pair of handcuffs. In Thailand, probably no one would accost you because he or she is *avoiding* you if you sit in a 'loose' position. This aspect refers mainly to women, obviously.

"Loose?" Meaning your feet are pointing east and west while your undies point north, or directly into a looker's eyes. This is considered indecency from good old tradition point of view and should be avoided. Likewise, very short shorts showing too much thigh flesh is not, to be frank, welcomed at all. You might not agree, we know, but you are not in the 'high' class level in local eyes.

Many times in buses, the driver is distracted by unconscious poor sitting of female passengers in the few front seats. It is hard to look both at the road and the mirror to steal some glances of exposed knickers at the same time. (Perhaps there should be squint-eyed drivers, you might suggest. But then, the bus will be going where he is looking instead of he looking where the bus should be going!).

DO NOT LIP-KISS

This has already been mentioned but we say it once more in case you missed the other section. No Thai will kiss his spouse goodbye in public even if the parting would be for many long years. Please try not to break this healthy tradition of the locals. You could, and still maintain your honour, give your spouse (not a local), a peck at the cheek as a meeting/parting gesture. You probably would receive smiles of approval and nods of appreciation, instead of frowns of frustration. And somehow, contempt. (You could do your homework first before going to the airport!!).

We hope you recall the 'Don't' in our Introduction.

Be very careful on...

RENTALS

Many visitors and residents will rent some vehicular contraptions for either serious use or pleasure.

At resorts, the usual rentals are jeeps, motor-cycles, boats or sea scooters. The past high number of misfortunes prompted this section to be included, which has nothing to do with tradition. Economic opportunists tempted by greed for money has ruined many otherwise pleasant holidays and caused a few lives. Be very alert when renting anything.

DO REMEMBER that many vehicles at holiday resorts do not have a third party insurance coverage. Taking one is taking a big risk for some machines are not road worthy. In an accident, you pay.

DO CONFIRM with the owner as to who will pay should there be a mechanical breakdown that requires a hefty repair bill. He will argue you do, since the insurance, if any, will cover lost or accident only. A breakdown, some pre-set, is not an accident.

DO REALISE that it is a traffic offense not to display the number plates. Some vehicles have none at the front and/or back. If they can do it, it does not mean you can. Check this when renting a machine.

DO NOT rent a vehicle from anyone who claims he is the owner, unless it is quite obvious, like in a rental office and others can be seen signing forms, taking delivery, etc.

DO NOT LEAVE the rented vehicle unlocked for a long time/out of sight. There had been cases when the owner robs his own machine and then happily waits for you to show up. You know the consequences if this happens.

DO CHECK VITAL mechanical parts *in the presence of the renter* so that if anything should fall off just as you touch it, you will not be blamed, i.e. having to pay for it. Check: brakes (foot and hand); tyres including the spare for 4-wheeled vehicles; head, tail, side and signal lights. Check, in fact, every other thing you feel should be looked over.

RENTALS

DON'T LET ANY stranger borrow the vehicle even for a moment. The reasons are not hard to guess for the more seasoned. For the 'nice clean' fellow, here's why: some parts may be changed; a duplicate key could be machined in a jiffy; he could get into an accident. The best of reasons: you may never see the vehicle again though you may or may not see him once more. (A lady had to skip out of the country because she could not raise enough money for a replacement after losing her motor-cycle. Her name is probably on the police wanted list).

DO KNOW YOU have to pay for the FULL price of the rented vehicle if it is lost during your care. This has been the practice for ages. Do check with the owner as the condition may/may not be stated in the written contract.

DON'T SIGN ANYTHING in Thai. If he does not have it in English at all, he can find himself another potential victim.

DON'T BE DULY shocked if you are asked to deposit your passport as an assurance while the vehicle is in your possession. This is the normal practice and so far no known case of abuse has been known or reported.

DO KNOW THAT an International Driving Permit is officially required but, well..., during peak period, well... *But* if an accident involves a serious injury and you have no licence or it has expired, well... they do permit visitors to model prisoners during non-visiting hours!

SOME USEFUL THAI PHRASES

I want to rent a car / motor cycle	*phom tongkarnchao rot / moto-sai*	ผม ต้องการเช่า รถ/มอเตอร์ไซด์
I have an international driving permit	*phom mi bai anuyat kup khi sakon*	ผมมีใบ อนุญาตขับ ขี่สากล
How much per day?	*wan nuen tho-rai*	วันหนึ่งเท่าไหร่
Where is the petrol station?	*pump narm mun yu thinai*	ปั้มน้ำมัน อยู่ที่ไหน
Do you have a good road map?	*mi phaen-thi dee dee mai*	มีแผนที่ดีดีไหม
The tank is empty	*thang mai mi nam manh*	แท็งค์ไม่มี น้ำมัน
The front light is out	*fai-na mai tit*	ไฟหน้าไม่ติด

149

Making it out at...

<u>RESTAURANTS</u>

This is the easiest place to get irritated, annoyed, angry, frustrated, even disgusted and every other form of being 'hot up' when something goes wrong; and things will go wrong, by western standard of waitering and service almost every time a visitor goes for dinner!

Knowing some facts of life, Thai style, will go a longer way than remembering a few 'don'ts.'

If you would agree that the idea of going to a restaurant is to enjoy the food and atmosphere and not to be frustrated then success is not impossible. If you feel that because you have the money and you are paying the asking price and thereby deserves to be treated 'right' then the word 'success' does not even arise, let alone its probability! Mark the words ENJOY and RIGHT.

What is 'right' to you may not be necessarily so to the restauranteur or humble waiter - right? For instance, if the cook takes a long time, your scolding the waiter is injustice to him.

The first thing to note is that Thais do not rush things or become frantic the way Westerners are used to. The second thing is to exercise patience.

DO KEEP YOUR COOL — KEEP YOUR VOICE DOWN

To begin on the right footing to eating, the first thing to do in any restaurant is to keep the voice down, in ordering, in talking, in paying and in departing. Loud voices equal bad manners. Your voice is 'loud' if the next table can hear you. Can you hear theirs? Hopefully, no.

DO EXERCISE PATIENCE

Next thing is to remember that the waiter may not come immediately if he/she is on the way to somewhere else. After an indication to come, the very waiter may seem to have disappeared forever. You could have waved your hand rudely in his eyes or more likely, she just does not bother to acknowledge and simply would not show up. Many are not well paid at cheap restaurants and are over-worked.

DO BECKON CORRECTLY

The proper way to beckon is to place the palm down and wave your fingers (facing the floor) rapidly. The reverse of palm up is not polite, nor of snapping the fingers.

The simplest way is to catch a passing waiter and call out **'nong'** (= sister or brother) with perhaps a raised hand, accompanied by, if possible, a half smile. He or she will either acknowledge and return later or stop dead to hear you.

DO SPEAK SLOWLY AND CLEARLY

As even English-speaking waiters are awkward in the language, you should *speak extra slowly and clearly* especially when ordering food. It is best if you simply point at the number in a menu and say "45 - one, please;" or "33 - two, please."

DO SHOW TOLERANCE

The remarkable dining etiquette of the Thais is tolerance. You will hardly hear a Thai complain loudly about the fly in his soup or demanding to see the manager or "I told you I do NOT want garlic," etc. Thais go to a restaurant to enjoy. If conditions are not up to expectations they try to compromise, like going over to another table and politely asking the other diner if a chair may be taken away, and then, usually, taking it himself. They don't normally stand still and then order a waiter to fetch another chair.

When it comes to paying the bill, the best choice of words is "*nong, chek bin*" when in a restaurant, not eating houses or roadside stalls. Translated it amounts to 'check my bill please.' This is one instance when an older and higher-in-status person could use the sentence roundup word *krup (ka* if you are a lady) without losing dignity. This is politeness here.

In shops and at stalls say, "*kit tang*" or "*kep tang.*" Either term is the usual way to address a waiter or the cook himself to have your 'bill' cleared. The first expression means "calculate money" and the latter means "collect money." You will sometimes hear someone says "kep tang duay." It still means the same thing but *duay* means 'also.' The whole implication means, in our thinking, "please collect your money also, apart from cooking the nice food for me."

"I'LL GET IT!" VERSUS: "WHAT'S MY SHARE OF THE BILL?"

In Thailand, the inviter to a meal automatically pays the full bill. Going Dutch is not common and is an insult to the one who calls you for dinner. If you call a group of Thais out, you foot the whole bill likewise. Many big restaurants accept one form of credit card or other.

If you try to chip in, you will find that you will be politely declined.

DO CHECK YOUR BILL FIRST

Sometimes your full bill includes those items you subsequently cancelled when you decided to make a switch. It might also include items you never ordered, or ordered but never came.

TO TIP OR NOT TO TIP?

Tipping is **not** expected outside hotel restaurants but any waiter would appreciate a small token, like ten or twenty baht. You need not go the usual 10 percent level as in the West.

Our suggestion is to go by ear: if you are truly happy with service and food, why limit to just a ten percent level? If you are not, why give even ten baht?

HOW TO ANSWER *'AROY MAI?'*

If you are in the company of any local, nine out of ten times, he or she will ask you if your particular dish/food is *'aroy mai'* meaning "delicious or not?" The favoured and right answer is to say *'aroy'* or *'aroy mak'* delicious; (yes), very delicious even if it is not quite to your expectation.

The Westerner does not normally ask "is it delicious?" for every item of a meal in the course of a dinner. But Thais like to hear that something is nice and delicious and since there are also many versions to a particular food, the observer or host would like to know if you are served well, that is, whether the cook has done his best for you. It happens so often that some foreigners get bored hearing the expression without knowing why.

USEFUL THAI EXPRESSIONS

DO TRY to use the following phrases for better understanding:

Pepsi-Cola	*pep-see*	แป๊บซี่
Coca-Cola	*kho-laa*	โคล่า
Sanwiches	*san-wit*	แซนด์วิซ
Water	*nam*	น้ำ
Ice	*nam kaeng*	น้ำแข็ง
Coffee	*kar-fae*	กาแฟ
Tea	*cha*	ชา
Hot	*ron*	ร้อน
Hot coffee / tea	*karfae / cha ron*	กาแฟ/ชาร้อน
Beer	*biar*	เบียร์
Cool/cold	*yen*	เย็น
Cold beer	*biar yen*	เบียร์เย็น
Very cold beer	*biar yen yen*	เบียร์เย็น เย็น
Pepper	*prik thai*	พริกไทย
Fish (soy) sauce	*nam plah*	น้ำปลา
Salt	*kleur*	เกลือ
Do not put sugar	*mai sai namtan*	ไม่ใส่น้ำตาล

One more glass	*ik kaew nueng*	อีกแก้วหนึ่ง
One more coffee	*karfe ik kaew nueng*	กาแฟอีกแก้วหนึ่ง
One more bottle	*ik kuat nueng*	อีกขวดหนึ่ง
I did not order this	*chan mai dai sang*	จานนี้ผมไม่ได้สั่ง
Will you accept credit card?	*rup kredik kard mai*	รับเครดิตการ์ดไหม
I am hungry	*phom hiew*	ผมหิว
I want to eat Thai food	*phom tongkarn tharn aharn Thai*	ผมต้องการทานอาหาร ไทย
Do you have the menu in English?	*mi menu phasa Angkrit mai*	มีเมนูภาษาอังกฤษไหม
A table for two people	*toh samrab song khon*	โต๊ะสำหรับสองคน
The food must not be very hot (spicy)	*aharn mai tong phed maak*	อาหารไม่ต้องเผ็ดมาก
Please bring a large bottle of beer	*khaw bier yai nueng khuat*	ขอเบียร์ใหญ่หนึ่งขวด
I'd like to change my order	*phom khaw plian aharn thi sang*	ผมขอเปลี่ยนอาหารที่สั่ง
What would you suggest?	*khun wa chah sang arai di*	คุณว่าจะสั่งอะไรดี
I don't know what to order	*phom mai saab chah sang arai di*	ผมไม่ทราบจะสั่งอะไรดี

Bring me salt and pepper	*kan phrik thai kleua*	ขอพริกไทย กับเกลือ
Bring me another pair of fork	*khaw shonn- somm ik*	ขอช้อน ซอมอีก
and spoon	*nueng khou*	หนึ่งคู่
I don't want to eat anymore	*phom mai tharn a-rai ik laew*	ผมไม่ทาน อะไรอีกแล้ว
May I have the bill, please?	*check bin (for restaurant) kep tang (non-restqautant)*	เช็คบิล เก็บตังค์
That was a good meal	*a-harn aroi mak*	อาหารอร่อยมาก
Please give me (a cup of) hot tea	*khaw cha ronn*	ขอชาร้อน
Please give me strong hot coffee	*khaw kafae ronn kae-kae*	ขอกาแฟร้อน แก-แก
Please give me black iced coffee	*khaw owe-liang (or) kafae dam-yen*	ขอโอเลี้ยง หรือ กาแฟ ดำเย็น
Give me another glass	*khaw ik nueng*	ขออีกหนึ่ง แกว
Give me another bottle	*khaw ik kaew nueng*	ขออีกหนึ่งขวด
Give me a receipt	*khaw bai-set*	ขอใบเสร็จ

Hints for your...

<u>SHOPPING</u>

This is an exciting exercise: it is exciting to the seller and an exercise for you. While you are looking the good over the seller is sizing you up. In the end, you will be excited to know you have overpaid by a wide margin.

This is one activity, shopping, where practically every one indulges in. The hints here pertain to expensive/valuable merchandise, which no buyer would like to feel to have been cheated.

Unfortunately, this happens, especially to tourists.

DO BE AWARE OF IMITATIONS. Asian countries are noted for piracy and Thailand is probably the champion! You name it, we have it, imitations.

Those T-shirts, wallets, shoes, watches and most brand name goods may even look more genuine than the genuine.

DO BE CAREFUL with diamonds. They may be cut glass; ha,ha,ha. Buy only from reliable dealers who are prepared to offer 'chopped and signed' receipts, stating the full value of the goods. If, upon return, it is found that they are glass, report to the Tourism Authority of Thailand or the Thai Embassy if there is one in your city.

If the seller is genuine, he would be prepared to include if you ask, that the money is fully refundable if the good is fake. But be careful: he could deny that the good was not his and that YOU try to outsmart him by switching.

Now what?!

DO BE ALERT of handicrafts or porcelain declared as 'antique.' The antique period may only be a few months. The goods could have been buried with chemicals or exposed to the sun and rain and tampered with to make them look old. They know how to do it; we do not know how to explain it.

DO BE AWARE that in some places, you could be paying very high prices. Some truly disgraceful sellers simply top up their selling prices when Caucasians show irresistible interest.

Pretend to be interested at length on something you hate, casually enquire on those you love

and then say "maybe I'll come back tomorrow." He might just take the bait and sell it/them to you at good bargains because he thinks you won't return tomorrow. It's a cat and mouse game but wouldn't you want to save say, two thousand baht? Or at least feel proud you are the winner of the oral tug-of-war?

DO EXPECT second grade quality if you pay second grade prices. In this country no clear distinction is made and a shopper might end up with a top piece where a button would fall off easily or an attachment, like a sleeve, was not stitched on fully. Many seemingly perfect pieces are actually 'seconds' or rejects for export due to almost undetectable faults. Some of these made their way to respectable department stores or mediocre boutiques.

DO REMEMBER THAT if you request for something valuable to be sent to your home, you may end up with a fake duplicate. Trust yourself insofar as delivery is concerned.

DO TRY TO KEEP an eye on your credit card all the time. If possible, request for it to be endorsed in front of you, not in a back room where the operator is out of sight for a long time. If this happens, suspect some foul play. For safety sake, prevent such possible ideas by a staff by requesting it machined 'here' before he/she can move to a back room. Say something stupid like, "I want to see how you do it. I've never seen it done!" And look serious.

SHOPPING

DO BARGAIN DOWN prices if you fancy something from the many roadside stalls or bargain bazaars. These sales sharks may sell at double the price of that of a department store. A local friend accompanying is only good in so far as interpreting goes; the seller will ask your friend why he is siding you to cut him down. At times it is better to go alone for you can somehow pretend you are not that new while a Thai person doing the talking is a clear giveaway.

SOME USEFUL WORDS & EXPRESSIONS

English	Thai (romanized)	Thai
I want to go	*phom / chan*	ผม/ฉัน
shopping	*chah pai ha*	จะไปหา
	sue khong	ซื้อของ
Do you want to come along?	*pai duay-kan mai*	ไปด้วยกันไหม
What time do the stores open?	*pok-kati raankha*	ปกติร้านค้า
	perd ki mong	เปิดกี่โมง
May I see that?	*khaw phom*	ขอผม
	dou anh nanh	ดูอันนั้น
Do you have other colours	*si uen mi mai*	สีอื่นมีไหม
How much is it altogether?	*ruam-kanh*	รวมกัน
	thang-mod	ทั้งหมด
	thao rai	เท่าไหร่
I'll buy it if it is cheaper	*phom chah sue*	ผมจะซื้อ
	tha lod dai ik	ถ้าลดได้อีก
Is it colour fast?	*si tok mai*	สีตกไหม
Do you have it in red	*si daeng mi mai*	สีแดงมีไหม

Do you have it in grey / purple / ivory / jade green	*si thaow mi mai si muang / si nga shaang / si khiao yok*	สีเทา/มีไหม สีม่วง สีงาช้าง สีเขียวหยก

SOME COMMON VOCABULARY

bag for travelling	*krapaow dernthaang*	กระเป๋า เดินทาง
bathing suit, costume	*choud waai-nam*	ชุดว่ายน้ำ
bedsheets	*pha pou thi-nonn*	ผ้าปูที่นอน
brassieres	*seua yok-song*	เสื้อยกทรง
cosmetics	*khreuang sam-arng*	เครื่อง สำอางค์
very expensive	*phaeng maak*	แพงมาก
electrical goods	*khreuang shai fai-fah*	เครื่องใช้ ไฟฟ้า
insecticides	*ya kha-malaeng*	ยาฆ่าแมลง
perfume	*narm-homm*	น้ำหอม
scissors	*kan-krai*	กรรไกร
stationery	*khreuang khian*	เครื่องเขียน
underwear	*shoud shan nai*	ชุดชั้นใน
Thai silk shirts	*shirt mai Thai*	เชิ้ตไหมไทย
Thai umbrella	*rom Thai*	ร่มไทย
Thai-costumed dolls	*touk-kata shoud Thai*	ตุ๊กตาชุด ไทย

phaeng maak

165

When you take a dip in....

SWIMMING

We have expanded this section to include areas and advice that might seem naïve to you but it is hoped, will prove to be a reminder if not anything else.

Swimming will usually take place at either a hotel swimming pool (as foreigners hardly visit public pools), a waterfall pool, the sea and, in the outskirt villages, in a stream, river or pond.

Women should take some precautions and nothing for granted.

DON'T SWIM NAKED, AT ANY TIME

One can never tell when somebody might show up. Nudity, partial or total, is immensely frowned upon in the whole country for it reflects complete discourtesy. No local would like to see a man/woman naked on the beach, although his instincts would drive him to look. He will look and probably say to himself, "that person is like an animal, no respects for himself/herself." Even if you don't care about such comments, a woman could get into some nasty trouble if the beach is lonely and in a remote place. In short, she could be harassed, to disguise another word. Does any woman want that? The consequence might be such that you would not be able to refer to what has been said in this passage, ever, again.

DON'T SUNBATHE TOPLESS, EVEN IF YOU ARE ONLY SUNNING YOUR BACK

Apart from displaying an unpleasant sight a woman is inviting the same problem as swimming naked in a quiet beach. The exception is the hotel pool where the staff has been well trained to accept this behaviour and the place is too private (public) for impolite advances. A bare-chested woman anywhere here is still considered of 'low class' distinction. The emphasis is again on possible injury to yourself, initiated by you.

Sometimes a Thai woman is seen semi-naked at popular beaches. This is an occupation hazard a service girl has to endure if her foreigner companion insisted she take off her top.

THE SEA

This is the area with the most drownings. Police do not or will not reveal the actual deaths per season but those who have been residing at coastal resorts will have an indication through word of mouth. Check up on your Travel Book for some details but there are authority notices at beaches giving dates for suggested non- swimming periods.

A 'must' to follow is May to October for Phuket, Koh Samui and particularly outlying islands off these islands that are very popular with divers.

DO OBSERVE THE red flag warning when it is hoisted. Some big hotels fail to do this. It means no swimming at all. What about wading, say, just ten feet from the waves? This could be dangerous because there may be a steep drop-off which could mean a strong unseen under current.

DON'T LEAVE VALUABLES unattended on the shore, especially if a deck chair is not rented. (Why bring along valuables except for the video or camera?)

DON'T SWIM NEAR rocky headlands. Sea snakes are more poisonous than their land cousins. A swimmer may see none for months but observe two gliding about the next day.

DON'T touch any jelly fish you know nothing of - even those washed ashore or discarded by fishermen.

DO be on the look out for jet scooters. For this reason, do swim within the float enclosure provided by bigger hotels.

OTHER PLACES

DO WATCH OUT for fresh water snakes in forest streams, jungle rivers and farmland canals when you go for a dip at some village. Some still-water ponds and wells abound with them in addition to all sorts of other creepy crawlies.

DO REMEMBER THAT the cool, clean surface of a waterfall pool may conceal a sharp boulder tip just where you think is a good diving spot. Sadly, Thailand still lacks thousands of warning signs where there should be.

DO NOT POLLUTE a running stream as there may be villagers downstream who depend on this water for almost everything.

DO WATCH OUT, ladies, for Peeping Toms. You do not want to turn them into rapists and from rapists, to murderers. Ladies must realise that nearly all local village males have never been with a white girl before and for one to tempt them unconsciously at their home ground is asking for the maximum. A man might perhaps understand the implication here better. It's the other chapter of sex education, to let you read between the lines.

GENERAL

1. Do not swim in the sea after a heavy meal. It's the sea, not you.

2. Do not force a Thai girl to the water. Many are either poor or non-swimmers, unlike a typical foreign girl who is adapt at many sports. Many grow up without a single day's experience in a gym, court or pool.

3. Don't litter the beach. It can be seen that some so-called 'more educated' foreigners lose out to an illiterate vendor. If you have a local with you, you would have diminished your own reputation.

4. Do not embrace one another while lying on the sand. A local might wait to see what's the next act in this 'free show.' It could be a nasty experience for the lady next time she is alone and recognised.

Embarking on...

TOURING AND TREKKING

Most, if not all, visitors will embark on sight-seeing. Sometimes, accidents do happen. The following precautionary advice mixes cultural and routine characteristics.

CONDUCTED TOURS

DO NOT EXPECT things to be what they are in Europe or USA just because it is a professional paid tour. Take-off time could be delayed; a mini-bus appears instead of a super-coach as advertised and destinations might have to be altered due to all kinds of reason. In a way, be prepared for 'adventure' from the sense of change. In another, in the real sense, some conducted tours are just a shade better than daylight swindle.

DO INFORM SOME authority, like the Tourism Authority if you really feel cheated from some changes in itinerary. This does happen. Keep details, printed brochures, tour itinerary, ... everything.

DO KNOW THAT there are many independent guides who are not supposed to be guides because they could be foreign workers out for some moonlighting income. Their rates are lower but as they are untrained and unauthorised they might comply with, for instance, your request for a short cut while hiking. You might just end up being chased by some wild animal.

DO GULP DOWN a couple of travelling sickness pills beforehand if you are sensitive to shakes. Many drivers here don't drive - they just put the gear in and roar away at breakneck speed. Also, certain roads in way-out countryside are more suited for bulldozers and tanks.

DO ASK FOR details of the tour, especially if it is a long haul to provinces. If things are different from what you are told, you

might not get a refund. The operators have enough reasons to counter any objection. When you are satisfied, then book the tour. Be prepared for this.

DO NOT REQUEST for a 'near the front' seat (or sit in front) if you can't stand loud blaring noises from a TV screen that could be right in front of you. Check if there are such things first in a bus.

DO BEWARE of some tour guides. Some are hardly 'professional.' In fact, they can be crooks! They might insist that certain shops offer gifts of a life time. What they do not say is "I will not get my commission if you don't buy from here."

PERSONAL SIGHT-SEEING

Sometimes it might be better to tour a place on your own if 1) you are young, strong and have a companion as well; 2) you know for sure you can take the rough and tough aspects of any tropical country road or forest; 3) you are prepared 'for anything.' There are the pros and cons of doing it by yourself but you must be fully alert all the time. The only thing is, you accept total responsibility for any mishap. Not advisable. Backpackers, especially females, should be extremely careful. Many caves are unexplored and if you are lost in one of them, you might not *be found*. Just-qualified 'divers' should be humble enough to go through minute details with their buddies. Just-passed 'drivers' should remember driving here, with some exceptions, is dangerous because there are many bus/truck drivers who take pills to keep awake.

DO NOT FORGET to find out when is the last bus/taxi/boat back if you are planning a one-day trip. Ask around first as sign boards can be outdated or transport operators could switch things round a bit to fit their own interest.

DO NOTE THAT when you take an overnight air-conditioned coach to a distant place like from Bangkok to Chiang Mai or Phuket, Hat Yai or elsewhere, a free midnight snack at some midway bus terminal is included. The blue (or other) copy of your ticket is your coupon for the snack. Many Caucasians who cannot read Thai are not aware of this privilege. Try it. You cannot miss this one as the bus makes only one stop between midnight and two am when the conductress makes the only announcement but in Thai.

DO NOT CAMP anywhere you like just because you have your sleeping bag along. Certain places, like remote beaches with boulders may have poisonous snakes crawling out at night. Some beaches are out of bounds to visitors as they belong to the army, though there are no signs to warn you. Check up with your boatman or a villager first. Heard of Peeping Toms?

DO BE READY for a sudden rainfall anytime in this country.

DO BRING SOME insect repellent with you all the time. Notice that ordinary mosquito bites cause bigger swellings on Caucasians' skins than on locals.'

DO NOT CARRY too many 1,000 baht currency notes. It can be less bulky but it is more difficult to change or use.

DO NOT VENTURE to any remote beach, whatever the brochure says, if both are young women only. If you insist, be prepared for any trouble, mainly thefts when you go swimming when your possessions had to be left on the shore. But be prepared for rape and strangulation in utterly remote beach, jungle, cave or waterfall.

DO MAKE SURE your motor cycle, if renting one, is really roadworthy. Check it out yourself. Do not take the owner's word for it.

TREKKING

DO NOT use a flash camera very near an elephant. The animal might appear docile but could be easily frightened by the flash and then goes wild. It's dangerous.

DO NOT touch any wild plant or flower that you do not know or is not commonly seen. Ask the guide if there is one.

DO NOT trek alone if possible. It is simply not wise. This includes 'safe' forest reserves. You might just be mistaken for big game by some poachers.

DO NOT SWIM in a river unless you are told it is safe. Have you ever heard of crocodile meat? Swimming in a waterfall pool is usually o.k.

DO BE PREPARED for insect or reptile bites. Wear proper shoes, be a real hiker in all sense. Check up on the notorious rainy season for that area before setting out.

DO NOT HITCH HIKE, if you are women, or accept a lift by men. You are inviting harm, almost certainly.

DO NOT TAKE any 'unbeaten path' which is not a path at all. In mountains, follow only well-used paths. Even these paths are often infested with snakes and scorpions.

DO TAKE NOTE that in the North, a favourite spot for hiking, hill tribes may not speak Thai at all as they have their own tongues. These people are generally shy, so shy that they will not want a photograph taken. Please do not insist. They may look dirty but they are very gentle and sensitive people.

While you are....
TRAVELLING

This is one area practically every tourist will fall into some kind of trap or get into a rip-off plan or ending up with more disappointment than pleasure.

The few points mentioned here are not complete as every journey may have its own problem at the start, during, or after the trip.

DO BE SUSPICIOUS of free offers, voluntary guides and unsolicited recommendations to shops. Reason: nobody does anything for free. Many scams abound.

DO REJECT ALL free offers of refreshments or food, especially in the train or overland coach. You might end up asleep!

DO HAGGLE AND HAGGLE with public transport owners everywhere. It is expected and is a way of life. To feel embarrassed is to spend extra money unnecessarily. This excludes scheduled commercial buses.

DO BE CAREFUL of acquaintances inviting you to any form of gambling, where, take it for granted, you might end up having to wire home for additional finances. For sure, you will never 'win' in the long run. Nor get away if you won and had other ideas.

DO TAKE YOUR bag containing important documents with you wherever you go, including to the washroom. Leaving it with your companion is totally unwise. Reason: someone could just distract him and an accomplice snatches your bag under his very nose!

DO CHECK YOUR change at all counters, be they currency booths or ticketing windows at bus terminals, movie houses or food centres. Many cashiers are good at making mistakes, to their advantage.

DO LOOK OUT for food that is stale. This is where most visitors are surprised. There is no active consumers' association to prevent abuses of things sold. Even supermarkets stock expired items sometimes, especially those in smaller towns.

DO INSIST METERED taxis turn on the reading as you get in. Often the driver 'forgot' to turn off the previous fare. If the driver refuses to turn the meter on, get out and pay nothing, for it means he will overcharge at journey's end. You can pre-agree on a fare before alighting if you know what you should pay.

THE AEROPLANE

DO RECONFIRM FLIGHT particulars since the off-season schedule could vary with peak period. The best thing to do, if you are not phoning up yourself (because of language problem), is to witness the actual call being made. Tour companies are notorious for this, resulting in confirmed seats being re-sold. Remember also courtesy may be unheard of at check-in counters.

DO NOT CARRY any package for anyone unless you know what is inside. You do not want to face the hangman upon arrival at another country. In Malaysia and Singapore, the penalty is mandatory death. Details can be checked up for permitted quantity for medical or personal reason with embassies.

THE TRAIN

DO LOOK UP official schedules for all kinds of details for inward journey and the non-stop trip to Malaysia. It is advisable to secure bookings before travel: 24 hours is an adequate leeway usually.

DO BEAR IN mind that train tickets may be sold while the train is fully booked. This is possible for certain short sectors. You may ask: Is there "standing only?" If there is, the clerk will still warn you there is no seating, in which case you agree and, upon getting the ticket, it will be noticed that the word 'Standee' is stamped or chopped on it. This means standing all the way throughout in theory but often, some people will get off at various stations and there will eventually be vacant seats, though perhaps not ajoining for two.

DO BE PREPARED to pay for what looks like a welcoming drink on the Bangkok-Padang Besar (Malaysia) run. A waitress will come by with a trayful of soft drinks before the train pulls out and ask, "Coke, orange?" Later she will come by again and say, "Twenty baht," or whatever the price is. Many first-timers have been taken.

DON'T PUT YOUR feet up on the backrest in front of you. Please see chapter on "Body Attributes."

THE BUS

DO BUY AN ADVANCE ticket if you can for air-conditioned coaches. For non-aircon, it's survival of the fittest at the counter prior to departure time.

Air-conned buses come in various 'classes'- V.I.P. with 24 seats and deluxe, super and what have you, with less leg room. All such air-con blue buses are comfortable with usually-polite conductresses for the entire journey. It's a sort of aeroplane on wheels.

DO SHOW YOUR passport and give your name when asked by the booking clerk. This is for insurance purposes in case of an accident.

DO ASK FOR a center or back seat if the TV at the front might prove too loud. Many overnight buses screen video tapes, all in Thai. Asking for the volume to be toned down can be asking for a nasty look with nothing happening. The concept of music-listening is a unique concept to the Thais: loud as thunder normally.

THE SELF-DRIVE

This is either a car, jeep or motor-cycle, of course. You cannot (not really) sail a yacht or fly an aircraft as yet in Thailand. There are helicopters for charter but we not talking along those expensive lines for this book.

DO KNOW THAT outside the super highways and main roads, signs are in Thai. It would be wise not to venture too far too late for the first time on a rented vehicle. You could be stranded in the middle of nowhere. With communication a probable problem and a lady at the back in some foul weather and no telephone about, it will be dangerous to pass the night.

DO MAKE SURE the contract permits the vehicle to go outside the territory or province. Unlike reputable companies, many machines are meant only for the area, e.g. you cannot drive from Chiang Mai to Bangkok legally.

DO CARRY A jerry can of fuel for any emergency. "Open twenty-four-hours" stations might not be opened!

DO NOT TRUST road maps explicitly. Thailand is progressing fast and some new roads are being opened or old ones becoming older and the tires will have to take some rally-type beating.

DO CHECK UP on weather conditions. No doubt this is common sense to seasoned drivers, but the rain can play havoc when typhoons strike. No real damage can be expected but the hazards can upset all your schedules.

DO NOT EXPECT supermarkets to stock items you take as common, e.g. cheese, frozen meats or ciders.

SOME USEFUL THAI PHRASES

These few words and sentences might be of help if you are without a guide. If you speak very slowly chances are you could be understood even though the tone in speaking could be slightly off, as it will be, anyway, even with many seasoned visitors. So, give it a shot if 'trapped' in a situation.

Where does this train go to?	*rot-fai ni pai nai*	รถไฟนี้ไปไหน
What time does the train leave?	*rot fai ork kee mong*	รถไฟออกกี่โมง
Is there a bus to Bangkok?	*mi rot mey pai Krungtep mai*	มีรถเมย์ไป กรุงเทพไหม
How much to Bangkok?	*pai Krungtep thow rai*	ไปกรุงเทพ เท่าไหร่
Please help me	*chuay phom noi*	ช่วยผมหน่อย
Stop. I want to get off here	*yout. jah long thi-ni*	หยุด จะลง ที่นี่
Where is the way out?	*thang ork yu thi-nai*	ทางออกอยู่ ที่ไหน
I am very tired	*if man:*	
	pom neui maak	ผมเหนื่อยมาก
	if lady:	
	chan neui maak	ฉันเหนื่อยมาก
Is there any drinking water	*mi nam duem mai*	มีน้ำดื่ม ไหม
Can this be eaten	*ni kin dai mai*	นี่กินได้ไหม

Is this seat taken?	*mi khon nang thi-ni laew rue yang*	มีคนนั่ง ที่นี่แล้ว หรือยัง
No, it's free	*yang mai mi*	ยังไม่มี
Do you smoke?	*khun soub buri mai*	คุณสูบ บุหรี่ไหม
Where will you get off?	*khun jak long thi-nai*	คุณจะลง ที่ไหน
I want to go to the lavatory	*phom / chan tongkarn pai hong-nam*	ผม / ฉัน ต้องการไป ห้องน้ำ
I'm here for only a day	*phom / chan mi vela you thi-ni wanh diao*	ผม / ฉัน มี เวลาที่นี่ วันเดียว
I'm here for two or three days	*phom / chan mi vela song-sarm wan*	ผม / ฉันมีเวลา สองสามวัน
Must I wait long?	*tong khoi naan mai*	ต้องคอยนาน ไหม
Is it far from here?	*klai maak mai*	ไกลมากไหม
Don't drive so fast	*ya khap reow*	อย่าขับเร็ว
Stop here	*yout thi-ni*	หยุด ที่นี่
I want to buy something	*phom / chan tongkarn sue khong*	ผม / ฉัน ต้องการซื้อ ของ
Wait a minute	*khoi sak-khrou nueng*	คอยสักครู่ หนึ่ง

When invited to a.....

WEDDING

Many Thai weddings of the upper middle class tend to swing towards the western style. Wedding gowns, tuxedos, hotel receptions, the tiered cake, champagne.

However, this is one ceremony that has variations and even among hill tribes some things are done differently.

Happily, there aren't many serious customs that a stranger can break, except for one: you don't kiss the bride!

DO JOIN IN all the fun should you be invited to any wedding. So long as you remember about not touching any lady or putting your feet everywhere and all that, there is nothing much to be conscious about.

DO TRY TO SIT on the floor if your friend is a poor country boy or girl. Don't accept the only chair around, because your head would then be higher than some elderly people. This would be impolite.

DO NOT EXPECT any wild drinking. 'Thais do not get drunk on such occasions.

DO NOT FEEL out of place if, for men, you do not have your suit handy. Except for the 'modern' church-types, you will feel more comfortable if you dress as everybody else. Best thing to do is to ask the bride or groom-to-be beforehand.

DO PRESENT THE happy couple with a small monetary token, if you like, but not in a white envelope as this colour would be more appropriate for a sad occasion. These days, money is more preferred to gift items.

This section, gentlemen, is:

MAINLY FOR WOMEN

This section is more for reading pleasure to add some insight into the way Thai women do or don't do a few things that may appear odd to the average visitor.

MAINLY FOR WOMEN

The typical Thai woman, vis-a-vis a 'modern office executive 'or' one conscious of status,' does not:

-carry an umbrella when it is hot. It's the rain that might spoil her hair-do. (Wonder why though).

-push a child in a perambulator.

-talk loudly. She is, most times, shy and reserved and always, soft spoken.

-smoke. Smokers are either trying to copy their western parts or they work in sex-related service trade.

They do not reach out for a stick or bottle to calm nerves. The lone foreign visitor woman should bear in mind that she can be subjected to some miserable experience.

The biggest offense now being done to Thais by foreign women is that the body is not well covered up or the dress is too transparent. The other is engaging in some 'distasteful' (to the Thais) embraces and kisses in public. Such actions are not accepted here. It is not that the modern Thai girl is not broadminded. It is that she wants to treasure her values that have been thoroughly ingrained into her system since childhood.

The total opposite: bar and a-go-go dancers. The behaviour of these girls is, quite definitely, shocking to even the western girl. (One reason why so many males visit Thailand?) This should provide one more 'Do' for the foreign woman:

DO MAKE SURE your mate has not engaged in unprotected sex with a service girl. You might contract HIV from him. Against what the authorities may say about the presence of AIDS, it is no secret that Thailand is not that safe; and this book is to be as frank as possible for you, regardless!

DO NOT TRUST anyone so easily, including one of the same sex.

DO NOT ACCEPT any consumable durable already opened, unless it is opened before your eyes. The Tourism Authority of Thailand has inserted this warning in publications and elsewhere. This advice is not good enough, for a cigarette pack could be resealed. The one stick you take could be designed for you. This is the easiest opening for a good-for-nothing to entice western women smokers.

It follows therefore that women who stay alone with locals, such as foreign exchange students, can become easy prey.

DO MAKE SURE your purse is tucked in well in your shoulder bag in a bus. If you are standing in a crowded bus, you could lose a few things. Sadly, if a timid Thai sees a though 'gangster' whisk or lift a foreigner's bag, he is not going to play boy scout.

Rambling about in...

ZOOS, PARKS &
AMUSEMENT FLOORS

*Believe it or not, some shopping complexes used to take pride in
confining animals in the uppermost floors. A couple of these
indoor Zoos still exist in Bangkok but pressure, fire and growing
concern for flora and fauna has all but kill this setup.*

*If visitors with children want to give the future adults some fun,
many ultra-big and ultra-ultra modern shopping complexes have
electrical gadgets and computerised fun items.*

DO LEND THIS country a hand when visiting public places in not defacing, damaging or destroying anything. It would be so beautiful for a young local child to see a foreigner making good use of proper disposal recepticles. This is so much needed at beach resorts, recreational and national forest parks when plastic bottles and bags are flung about.

DO BE SELECTIVE when buying food and drinks from vendors around recreation park boundaries. These people will have little water for washing and some food may just give you that stomach ache you don't need. It is no secret some of the food is dirty.

DO SAY 'NO' to offers of sale of stuffed animals, ivory tusks or animal-skin goods from shops or itinerant peddlars.

DO SAY 'NO' to offers of sale of live baby animals, especially when in the provinces where animals are cruelly caught. A cute harmless monkey is here because its mother first had to be shot to death and the little chap has to survive the fall from a tree and suffer untold (naturally) misery before we can see it in its chains, sack, basket or cage, usually minus a cup of water and soiled with rotten food around.

DO SAY 'NO' to all food items that are clearly meat of protected species of wild life. In fact, do boycott such restaurants completely even when your local friend suggests herbal turtle soup or a bear's paw that will give you that extra power. (Surely, one can do whatever one wants to do without 'that' extra [supposedly] power! How about 'practice makes perrfect' instead of resorting to doses of tiger's tooth, snake's bladdar or monkey's brain?)

DO SAY 'NO' to any suggestion by a total stranger; the earlier his attempt to strike up a conversation is cut short, the better.

ZIGZAGS

*These last few bits and pieces round up the Thai cultural
environment that you need to remember in order not to offend
any local unintentionally and to minimise or prevent discomfort to
yourself.*

*Some aspects are not cultural but are hints for your own safety
and personal enjoyment. A few points are repeated here as a
reminder and emphasis. Topics do not follow any order and may
'zig' from eating and 'zag' to something else and then 'zig' back
again to, say, country food.*

*Try to take things easy while you are here; formality and
protocol is not strictly observed usually.*

GIVE A THOUGHT

First, one should remember that the general local man may not be typically 'Bangkok Thai,' that is, he could be from the North, Northeast or South where his outlook may be entirely different.

The South, for example, has the most number of Muslims and if you invite one to a meal, he cannot eat pork nor should he drink any liquor. One good question to put across, if you are doing the ordering at any time, is to ask, 'Is there anything you don't eat, like pork maybe?'

The Northeast youngsters working in house-factories generally cannot speak 'Bangkok Thai' well. They tend to stay together and, if taken to a restaurant, will be confused by the array of forks, knives and spoons. In fact, they prefer sticky rice to the plain type and would have trouble handling even a fork and spoon. Many simply do not eat/have never eaten things considered usual in the West like cheese, mustard, corn flakes, salad dressings or macaroni.

DINING

DO ACCOMMODATE LIMITATIONS. Western food is alien to many and at buffet lunches, you will notice they are simply lost at European dishes. Generally too shy to ask, they will head straight for rice and top up with curry and vegetables they are familiar with.

DO MAKE SUGGESTIONS. Rather than ask what kind of wine he would like, it might be happier to say, "I'm having white wine with my fish; how about red for you, for your steak?" Beer is the easiest beverage with a first-time friend.

'EXCUSE ME, PLEASE'

There are only two phrases to get a message across:

'Khor thot' is used in all cases of seeking a pardon, equivalent to 'excuse me' in English except when someone is blocking your way and you want to pass through.

'Khor thang noi' is this exception. Because it means '(please) give me a little way (to pass through)'it is not used for other situations. You can still say 'khor thot' but it is not appropriate.

'GOOD MORNING / NIGHT'

Though there are equivalent words for these Thais do not use such terms. The general greeting/departing word *'sawatdee krup/ka'* is used in lieu of these greetings.

'WHERE ARE YOU GOING?'

The Thai phrase, *pai nai* often serves as a greeting word. The speaker is not trying to poke his nose into your affairs but 'where are you off to?' is akin to 'hello.'

The general response is *pai theow* meaning, 'for a stroll, for a spree around, nowhere in particular.' (In ancient China, it was -and still is, even here- 'have you eaten?' because upon seeing you, your friend would be happy to know that you had eaten, since famine was a problem then).

DON'T JUMP QUEUE

Many younger boys and girls are breaking this rule. At a public toilet, you should only head for the toilet you are waiting in front of. You cannot rush to an adjacent toilet just because you are also close to it when someone is obviously in that queue. You need to 'ask' for 'permission: 'May I go first please?'

This applies to anywhere where lining up is required, like at post offices, coupon booths, fast food counters or check out counters. Be prepared for a little 'rudeness' from a cashier who might signal to someone behind instead of attending to you first.

She might notice that the old lady behind has only two small items to clear against your trolley full of merchandise.

'LOSING FACE'

DO NOT CONTRADICT a comment in public. At a gathering, your friend makes a mistake and say, "Italy is the capital of Rome and I enjoyed my stay very much."

DO KEEP QUIET. SHUT UP! Everybody alert would know it's an insignificant error of speech. For anyone to correct the speaker and then giggle would tantamount to *insulting* him. Even privately, unless you know him well, let it pass, for he will still suffer from a loss of face! In the West, both speaker and listener would have had a hilarious time, and possibly pass it on to a third friend, just for kicks. It just doesn't work this way in Thailand. The conclusion may be sad: you will not make many friends with a 'jokeful' attitude. Thais are ultra-sensitive comparatively.

If you want to tell him he was wrong somewhere, give him one of the most stupid smiles you could come up with. After the speech, he might come up privately and ask you for that smile. Now you tell him that he got Rome and Italy mixed up, and you have won. Until his next speech!

NICKNAME

DO ASK IF his/her name is a nickname, if you want to, if introduced for the first time. Thais will not take offence at this but he/she might not be that willing to reveal the real name, that is, the one on the identity card; in which case press no further.

There are many reasons for Thais having nick names. One is that at birth some busybody old lady will pronounce that the newborn looks like a snake, a cat, a star or even a pig and start calling the child accordingly. This name eventually gets stuck to the baby. The other is that it is simply normal for a child to have a nickname which is almost always of one syllable and already commonly in use.

Thus, if you receive a phone call and the lady says she is Jum, or Lek or Kaeo you might have to ask for details if you already know five Jums and six Leks and cannot recognise the voice. Often, just the last syllable of a name is used, like "Orn" for 'Bungorn.' Try not be annoyed with the person, whatever the situation; it happens frustratingly to foreigners all the time but amusingly to locals.

BUS NUMBERS

DO NOTE when travelling internally by bus in Bangkok that although there are numbers, a same number bus may go to a different destination or half-way of its normal route you see on your map. The bus designation system is very confusing for a non-resident. Ask the conductor/conductress upon boarding.

DO BE CAREFUL when you have to stand in a bus, especially in non-airconditioned red or blue buses zig-zagging all over Bangkok. There have been cases of armed robbery and pick-pocketing, done with *finesse*.

WEDNESDAYS

DO TAKE NOTE that many shops close on Wednesdays. In up country, a whole street may be closed. This is due to some belief by traditional Thais that it is unlucky to engage in business or to just have a haircut on Wednesdays.

RUNAWAY DRIVER

DO NOTE THAT in a serious accident involving a heavy vehicle on a highway, the local driver will usually flee the scene. Stopping, getting down to render first aid and trying to get the injured to a hospital or even looking for a phone would be an extreme exception for the driver as he is normally a temporary worker, under pep pills to stay awake and he knows he will be sacked; apart from having no finance or insurance to compensate any party.

BEGGARS

DO NOT BE overly sympathetic to beggars anywhere. The government is trying to eradicate this and by giving your generous or whatever donations, you are indirectly feeding some organised gangs to buy more whiskey. If you must help, do buy the child or old woman some edibles.

ZIGZAGS

BOGUS OFFICERS AND FAKED ARTICLES

DO KNOW THAT there are many other fakes. Apart from these orphans who are under the control of some gangs who could be also controlling prostitutes, vendors, shop-owners and a host of other uncivil matters there are also bogus monks, bogus nuns, bogus policemen, dentists, charity workers complete with their paraphernalia, fortune tellers (by far the most), fishermen turned pirates, pirates turned fishermen...everything except, perhaps a bogus plane pilot (because he doesn't want to die! On second thought, maybe we do have them as well). For those thinking of employing locals, we also have faked certificates, doctored identity cards, forged passports, etc., etc. Enough for this paragraph!

LAW LAXITY

DO KNOW LAWS are not strictly enforced here and it takes a long time for any complaint to be investigated, by when of course, the bird would have flown. Laws change so often that enforcers lose track of the latest of the latest! A blatant bureaucratic sin is that when laws are changed, they are not always reported or announced widely if newspapers do not write about them. Often they are not handed down vertically to the lowest rank who really face the public so that it becomes a total waste of time making enquiries at some information window.

FALLACY OF TRAVEL BROCHURES

DO BEAR IN mind that many brochures are written by people who may have never been to the place they so beautifully describe. Such armchair work is unreliable but you have no way to tell. If you have to take chances, take intelligent risks. Word-of-mouth is one of the best sources while feature stories provide depth and more details. Short of all this, be ready for trial and error.

CANAL TAXIS

DO USE A long-tailed boat taxi especially in Bangkok as this cuts travelling time. Now there are safe wooden piers to board one of these banana-split things to a few major commercial points.

MAIL MISDIRECTION

DO NOT SEND any cash or important document where you have no other copy, by post, even if it is registered. The frequency of loss is not a joke. Also give plenty of time for a despatch to arrive at its destination - and we do mean *plenty*.

TAP WATER

DO NOT DRINK unboiled tap water anywhere. Bottled water comes in two categories: drinking water and mineral water.

BITES AND ILLNESSES

DO NOT IMAGINE that a dog bite is automactically rabid or when a mosquitoe stings, we will be malarial for sure. Some tourists are so paranoid that they carry all sorts of anti-illness pills. Many doctors in the west who prescribed all kinds of unnecessary capsules have never been here. They read prejudiced reports written by biased people and give you pills to make some extra money. If you can offord a holiday, you can afford to pay. There are just two likely areas that should cause some concern: stomach upset, due to spicy food and change of habits. And AIDS.

THE *FARANG* FIEND

DO BE REMINDED of a Dog Eats Dog situation, especially in Pattaya: that is, you can be fooled by your own kind with more disastrous results. Do not think only locals are "dangerous," using the word loosely. The sly Caucasians are not violent kidnappers or daring robbers but are quiet conmen looking for - to use a foul phrase, - any sucker; either sex, any age.

SPICY FOOD

DO MAKE SURE you have tried at least once, Thailand's most popular soup dish: the *tong yum koong*, meaning a spicy hot shrimp soup, usually served like the 'Chinese Steam Boat.' Not to have tried this is like missing out Fish & Chips in England or a Hamburger in the States. It's not only traditional, it's *the* thing to try.

BOOK BY ITS COVER

BE INFORMED THAT there are some books whose cover show captions in English but everything else inside is in Thai. Do not grab a couple in a hurry before the plane takes off, without flipping the inside over.

BRAND-NAME BODYWEAR

BE ALERT TO imitation products of popular names like Gucci, Dunhill, Lacoste, Polo, Wrangler, Ray Ban, etc. To take just one example: you can easily buy a dozen crocodile motifs for a few bahts from a roadside vendor and iron the logos onto your T-shirts yourself and Presto! You're a Lacoste Sports-shirt fan. Ha! Ha!

TO ROUND UP THE WHOLE IDEA:

DO BE ALERT, SMART AND CALM for anything and everything in Thailand - anywhere, anytime. More often, it is NOT the local's fault: it's the careless or unwise visitor's.

And finally, to quote a reminder that is basically aimed at ecotourism but nonetheless provides good food for thought for all good visitors:

Take nothing but photographs
Kill nothing but time
Leave nothing but footprints

IN A NUTSHELL

COOL MOUNTAINOUS NORTH

DO REFUSE an elephant ride if mammal appears about to drop dead due to overwork: overload, overwalk, with overfat people all over.

DON'T GO near Burmese borders. Gunners who cannot shoot straight might cause bullets to ricochet off their thick skins into your soft wallet. All the credit cards will be blown to bits!

DON'T TREK alone; or soon you will have fans with fancy ideas.

DO VISIT handicraft villages. Many are machine- crafted handicrafts. If you don't reveal this fact, your purchasing blunder can be concealed back home.

DON'T TAKE snapshots of cute native girls in native costumes unless unless prepared to pay 10-20 baht for their pose. They also know about roadway robbery. (They have tough guardians admiring you admiring them. Be careful).

THIRSTY NORTHEAST

DO POP by if time permits to this poorest region. Not only are farmers poor, their buffaloes, pigs, ducks, etc. etc. are also forever thirsty. I-saan, as region is called, is Dry Country.

DO RMEMEBER as place is still backward, everything else can be not forward. BUT, this makes for full gamut of surprises.

DON'T DISPLAY outward shocks at below subsistent level of living. They know they're poor and many feel ashamed of it.

DO TRY some Northeastern food. Typically: tom sum (papaya salad), kai yang (BBQ-ed chicken), khao neow (sticky rice). You may not like it but they love it. One man's meat...

METROPOLITAN BANGKOK

DON'T THINK too badly of the Capital. Just remember there are many *kinds* of angels with different *meanings* of smiles.

HISTORICAL CENTRAL

DO VISIT the many cultural and historical sites: ruins, restorations, remains.

DON'T FORGET there are many fairs & festivals in the region.

DO CHECK up with the Dept. of Fine Arts for serious in-depth, academic or study visit. They know and have interesting background facts.

EASTERN SEABOARD

DO ENJOY the many leisure facilites around Pattaya.

DO VISIT the many neighbouring islands. And go for the seafood.

DON'T LET smooth-talking conmen waltz you to bankruptcy.

DO HELP to keep beaches litter-free.

SEA-BREEZE SOUTH

DO NOTE sometimes the breeze is not there. It can be windless or stormy. But all beaches are inviting in southern islands.

DO BE advised that Phuket is the most expensive resort to date.

DON'T OVERPAY for anything. Bargain everything down, down, down. Don't be shy. Don't be afraid. Don't be taken in. Don't pay.

DO OBSERVE swimming warnings and be extremely on guard of motorised sea monsters: skiis, boats, half-boats.

DON'T BUY sea-shell/coral souvenirs. Very soon nothing will be left in the sea.

DON'T SNOOZE directly under a coconut tree full of nuts. So far, none has made a direct hit with smashing result lately. Can never tell....

KOH SAMUI

DO CHECK up on ferry crossing schedules/plane flight details from Bangkok, Pattaya or Phuket. Sometimes it's there; at times it's not!

FAR SOUTH   **DO KNOW** this is mainly Muslim territory: No consumption of pork in typically Islamic areas please.

DO NOT believe story of cheap smuggled goods near border towns. This is no longer true, most time. Police are doing a better job; smugglers having harder time, so goods become more expensive. Not worth the trouble looking.

PENANG

MALAYSIA

DO NOTE Thai Consulate now closes 3.00pm. and *coloured* photos needed for visa application/renewal.

DO MAKE sure when crossing border - no foreign packages inside your carelessly unzipped bag. Penalty for drug smuggling in Malaysia is automatic danggling until automatic stiffening.

DO ADJUST time forward by one hour.

Other **DOs & DON'Ts** series to be published by BB Publications

DOs & DON'Ts IN MALAYSIA

DOs & DON'Ts IN SINGAPORE

DOs & DON'Ts IN PHILIPPINES

DOs & DON'Ts IN MYANMAR

WATCH OUT FOR THEM!

COMMUNICATION GUIDES
FOR TRAVELLERS
AND RESIDENTS

PRACTICAL
VIETNAMESE
CHOU ONG BAR
a communication guide
for travellers and residents

PRACTICAL
MYANMAR
MINGALABA

15th Edition
PRACTICAL
THAI
SAWASDEE
a communication guide
for travellers and residents

THAI
HAWKER
FOOD

THAI
HAWKER
FOOD

- How to identify
- Where and When
- What makes up what
- Tips to remember
- Charts, Illustrations, ets.

BB
Publications